Poles

IN MINNESOTA

John Radzilowski

Foreword by Bill Holm

MINNESOTA HISTORICAL SOCIETY PRESS

For Kasia—Kocham Ciebie

Publication of this book was supported, in part, with funds provided by the June D. Holm-quist Publication Endowment Fund of the Minnesota Historical Society.

www.mnhs.org/mhspress

The Minnesota Historical Society Press is a member of the Association of American Univer-sity Presses.

Manufactured in Canada

1 2 3 4 5 6 7 8 9 01

International Standard Book Number: 1-615-15378-0

♾ The paper used in this publication meets the minimum requirements of the American National Standard for Information Sciences Permanence for Printed Library Materials, ANSI Z 39.48-1992.

Library of Congress Cataloging-in-Publication Data

Radzilowski, John, 1965–
    Poles in Minnesota / John Radzilowski ; foreword by Bill Holm.
        p.   cm. — (The people of Minnesota)
    Includes bibliographical references and index.
    ISBN 0-87351-516-1 (pbk.: alk. paper)
        1. Polish Americans—Minnesota—History. 2. Polish Americans—Minnesota—
    Social conditions. 3. Immigrants—Minnesota—History. 4. Minnesota—Ethnic relations.
    5. Minnesota—History. I. Title. II. Series.

F615.P7R33 2005
977.6'0049185—dc22

                                                                                    2004019301

This book was designed and set in type by Wendy Holdman, Stanton Publication Services, St. Paul, Minnesota; it was printed by Friesens, Altona, Manitoba.

Contents

Foreword

by Bill Holm

Human beings have not been clever students at learning any lessons from their three or four thousand odd years of recorded history. We repeat our mistakes from generation to generation with tedious regularity. But we ought to have learned at least one simple truth: that there is no word, no idea that is not a double-edged sword. Take, for example, the adjective *ethnic*. In one direction, it cuts upward, to show us the faces, the lives, the histories of our neighbors and ourselves. It shows us that we are not alone on this planet—that we are all rooted with deep tendrils growing down to our ancestors and the stories of how they came to be not *there*, but *here*. These tendrils are visible in our noses and cheekbones, our middle-aged diseases and discomforts, our food, our religious habits, our celebrations, our manner of grieving, our very names. The fact that here in Minnesota, at any rate, we mostly live together in civil harmony—showing sometimes affectionate curiosity, sometimes puzzled irritation but seldom murderous violence—speaks well for our progress as a community of neighbors, even as members of a civilized human tribe.

But early in this new century in America we have seen the dark blade of the ethnic sword made visible, and it has cut us to the quick. From at least one angle, our national wounds from terrorist attacks are an example of ethnicity gone mad, tribal loyalty whipped to fanatical hysteria, until it turns human beings into monstrous machines of mass murder. Few tribes own a guiltless history in this regard.

The 20th century did not see much progress toward solving the problem of ethnicity. Think of Turk and Armenian, German and Jew, Hutu and Tutsi, Protestant and Catholic, Albanian and Serb, French and Algerian—think of our own lynchings. We all hoped for better from the 21st century but may not get any reprieve at all from the tidal waves of violence and hatred.

As global capitalism breaks down the borders between nation-states, fanatical ethnicity rises to life like a hydra. Cheerful advertisements assure us that we are all a family—wearing the same pants, drinking the same pop, singing and going online together as we spend. When we invoke *family,* we don't seem to remember well the ancient Greek family tragedies. We need to make not a family but a civil community of neighbors, who may neither spend nor look alike but share a desire for truthful history—an alert curiosity about the stories and the lives of our neighbors and a respect both for difference—and for privacy. We must get the metaphors right; we are neither brothers nor sisters here in Minnesota, nor even cousins. We are neighbors, all us *ethnics,* and that fact imposes on us a stricter obligation than blood and, to the degree to which we live up to it, makes us civilized.

As both Minnesotans and Americans, none of us can escape the fact that we *ethnics,* in historic terms, have hardly settled here for the length of a sneeze. Most of us have barely had time to lose the language of our ancestors or to produce protein-stuffed children half a foot taller than ourselves. What does a mere century or a little better amount to in history? Even the oldest settlers—the almost ur-inhabitants, the Dakota and Ojibwa—emigrated here from elsewhere on the continent. The Jeffers Petroglyphs in southwest Minnesota are probably the oldest evidence we have of any human habitation. They are still and will most likely remain only shadowy tellers of any historic truth about us. Who made this language? History is silent. The only clear facts scholars agree on about these mysterious pictures carved in hard red Sioux quartzite is that they were the work of neither of the current native tribes and can be scientifically dated only between the melting of the last glacier and the arrival of the first European settlers in the territory. They seem very old to the eye. It is good for us, I think, that our history begins not with certainty, but with mystery, cause for wonder rather than warfare.

In 1978, before the first edition of this ethnic survey appeared, a researcher came to Minneota to interview local people for information about the Icelanders. Tiny though their numbers, the Icelanders were a real ethnic group with their own language, history, and habits of mind. They settled in the late 19th century in three small clumps around Minneota. At that time, I could still introduce this researcher to a few old ladies born in Iceland and to a dozen children of immigrants who grew up with English as a second language, thus with thick accents. The old still prayed the Lord's Prayer in Icelandic, to them the language of Jesus himself, and a handful of people could still read the ancient poems and sagas in the leather-covered editions brought as treasures from the old country. But two decades have wiped out that primary source. The first generation is gone, only a few alert and alive in the second, and the third speaks only English—real Americans in hardly a century. What driblets of Icelandic blood remain are mixed with a little of this, a little of that. The old thorny names, so difficult to pronounce, have been respelled, then corrected for sound.

Is this the end of ethnicity? The complete meltdown into history evaporated into global marketing anonymity? I say no. On a late October day, a letter arrives from a housewife in Nevis, Minnesota. She's never met me, but she's been to Iceland now and met unknown cousins she found on an Internet genealogy search. The didactic voice in my books reminds her of her father's voice: "He could've said that. Are we *all* literary?" We've never met, she confesses, but she gives me enough of her family tree to convince me that we might be cousins fifteen generations back. She is descended, she says with pride, from the Icelandic law speaker in 1063, Gunnar the Wise. She knows now that she is not alone in history. She has shadowing names, even dates, in her very cells. She says—with more smug pride—that her vinarterta (an Icelandic immigrant prune cake that is often the last surviving ghost of the old country) is better than any she ate in Iceland. She invites me to sample a piece if I ever get to Nevis. Who says there is no profit and joy in ethnicity? That killjoy has obviously never tasted vinarterta!

I think what is happening in this letter, both psychologically and culturally, happens simultaneously in the lives of hundreds of thousands of Minnesotans and countless millions of Americans. Only the details differ, pilaf, jiaozi, fry bread, collards, latkes, or menudo rather than vinarterta, but the process and the object remain the same. We came to this cold flat place so far from the sea in wave after wave of immigration—filling up the steadily fewer empty places in this vast midsection of a continent—but for all of us, whatever the reason for our arrival: poverty, political upheaval, ambition—we check most of our history, and thus our inner life, at the door of the new world. For a while, old habits and even the language carry on, but by the third generation, history is lost. Yet America's history, much less Minnesota's, is so tiny, so new, so uncertain, so much composed of broken connections—and now of vapid media marketing—that we feel a loneliness for a history that stretches back further into the life of the planet. We want more cousins so that, in the best sense, we can be better neighbors. We can acquire interior weight that will keep us rooted in our new homes. That is why we need to read these essays on the ethnic history of Minnesota. We need to meet those neighbors and listen to new stories.

We need also the concrete underpinning of facts that they provide to give real body to our tribal myths if those myths are not to drift off into nostalgic vapor. Svenskarnas Dag and Santa Lucia Day will not tell us much about the old Sweden that disgorged so many of its poor to Minnesota. At the height of the Vietnam War, an old schoolmate of mine steeled his courage to confess to his stern Swedish father that he was thinking both of conscientious objection and, if that didn't work, escape to Canada. He expected patriotic disdain, even contempt. Instead the upright old man wept and cried, "So soon again!" He had left Sweden early in the century to avoid the compulsory military draft but told that history to none of his children. The history of our arrival here does not lose its nobility by being filled with draft-dodging, tubercular lungs, head lice, poverty, failure. It gains humanity. We are all members of a very big club—and not an exclusive one.

I grew up in western Minnesota surrounded by accents: Icelandic, Norwegian, Swedish, Belgian, Dutch, German, Polish, French Canadian, Irish, even a Yankee or two, a French Jewish doctor, and a Japanese chicken sexer in Dr. Kerr's chicken hatchery. As a boy, I thought that a fair-sized family of nations. Some of those tribes have declined almost to extinction, and new immigrants have come to replace them: Mexican, Somali, Hmong, and Balkan. Relations are sometimes awkward as the old ethnicities bump their aging dispositions against the new, forgetting that their own grandparents spoke English strangely, dressed in odd clothes, and ate foods that astonished and sometimes repulsed their neighbors. History does not cease moving at the exact moment we begin to occupy it comfortably.

I've taught many Laotian students in my freshman English classes at Southwest State University in Marshall. I always assign papers on family history. For many children of the fourth generation, the real stories have evaporated, but for the Hmong, they are very much alive—escape followed by gunfire, swimming the Mekong, a childhood in Thai refugee camps. One student brought a piece of his mother's intricate embroidery to class and translated its symbolic storytelling language for his classmates. Those native-born children of farmers will now be haunted for life by the dark water of the Mekong. Ethnic history is alive and surprisingly well in Minnesota.

Meanwhile the passion for connection—thus a craving for a deeper history—has blossomed grandly in my generation and the new one in front of it. A Canadian professional genealogist at work at an immigrant genealogical center at Hofsos in north Iceland assures me, as fact, that genealogy has surpassed, in raw numbers, both stamp and coin collecting as a hobby. What will it next overtake? Baseball cards? Rock and roll 45 rpms? It's a sport with a future, and these essays on ethnic history are part of the evidence of its success.

I've even bought a little house in Hofsos, thirty miles south of the Arctic Circle where in the endless summer light I watch loads of immigrant descendants from Canada and the United States arrive clutching old brown-tone photos, yellowed letters in languages they don't read, the misspelled name of Grandpa's farm. They feed their information into computers and comb through heavy books, hoping to find the history lost when their ancestors simplified their names at Ellis Island or in Quebec. To be ethnic, somehow, is to be human. Neither can we escape it, nor should we want to. You cannot interest yourself in the lives of your neighbors if you don't take sufficient interest in your own.

Minnesotans often jokingly describe their ethnic backgrounds as "mongrel"—a little of this, a little of that, who knows what? But what a gift to be a mongrel! So many ethnicities and so little time in life to track them down! You will have to read many of these essays to find out who was up to what, when. We should also note that every one of us on this planet is a mongrel, thank God. The mongrel is the strongest and longest lived of dogs—and of humans, too. Only the dead are pure—and then, only in memory, never in fact. Mongrels do not kill each other to maintain the pure ideology of the tribe. They just go on mating, acquiring a richer ethnic history with every passing generation. So I commend this series to you. Let me introduce you to your neighbors. May you find pleasure and wisdom in their company.

Poles

IN MINNESOTA

The Michał Parulski family of Lincoln County, about 1914. Eight of the nine daughters in this family entered religious life as sisters. Rose Parulski (the little girl in the center) would become the first historian of her community, largely responsible for collecting many of the pictures in this book.

L ATE SUMMER 1905, Lincoln County, Minnesota. Michał Parulski paused and looked out over the heads of wheat nodding in the westerly breeze. These wheat fields, the pastureland, hayfields, and stands of oats were his: 240 acres in all. So much land! It would have been unimaginable back in the Polish village where he grew up. Only a lord would have owned so much. But now he, Michał, son of Jan and Katarzyna, thanks to the grace of God and years of toil, had his own fine patrimony that he could pass on to his sons and daughters.

The distant bells ringing the Angelus reminded him of the time, and he crossed himself and said a small prayer of thanks. To the southeast he could make out the steeples of St. John Cantius towering over the rolling, grass-covered hills, the church he and his neighbors had built. When he had arrived with his father and mother in the spring of 1884, the only church was a frame covered with shiplap whose walls shifted when the prairie wind blew fierce. All around there was an endless sea of grass broken here and there by dugout shanties made of thick sod. Now, there was a fine brick church with steeples that could be seen 20 miles away on a clear day and a Polish-speaking priest and nuns teaching in the school. Around the church in the little hamlet of Wilno there was a school, a rectory, a store, a smithy, and a saloon where folks could gather and read newspapers in Polish and talk about the weather and politics over a glass of beer.

How different it had been when they first arrived. People had wept with homesickness. Some packed up their families and went back east, calling this land a desert. Yet, many more had stayed and now—the bells ceased their ringing and brought his thoughts back to the work at hand. The day was not getting younger, and there was still much work to be done.[1]

Michał Parulski, his wife Katarzyna, and his parents Jan and Katarzyna, were one of the thousands of Polish families who have made a home for themselves in Minnesota over the past century and a half. Their descendants live in all areas of the state, north and south, urban, suburban, and rural, and in 2000 numbered nearly 260,000.[2] Although the largest number of these Minnesotans trace their history in the state to the great migrations of the late 19th and early 20th centuries, Polish immigrants have continued to arrive throughout much of the 20th century and even into the first years of the present century.

Polish immigration to Minnesota occurred in four broad categories:

- Settler immigrants, like Michał Parulski, who came, usually in family units, to find farms and homes, mostly in rural Minnesota, from the 1850s to the first years of 20th century.
- Labor immigrants, who began to arrive in the 1870s and came most heavily in the two decades before World War I. Seeking wage-labor jobs, these immigrants often arrived as individuals and settled mostly in urban areas and near the iron-mining and timber industries of northern Minnesota.
- Post–World War II arrivals who came after fleeing Nazi and Soviet persecution in the decade after 1945. Many were former victims of Nazi slave labor or concentration camps or Soviet gulags or were veterans of the Polish Armed Forces in exile who were unable to return home due to Soviet repression.
- Post-1965 arrivals who consist of three subgroups. First, a small number of economic refugees who were able to leave Communist-dominated Poland in the late 1960s and 1970s. Second, political refugees who escaped the Communist crackdown on

Counting Poles

Efforts to count the number of Polish Americans have been fraught with frustration for scholars. Because Poles who immigrated prior to 1918 came from a country that did not officially exist, they were often undercounted or miscounted. In 1900, for example, U.S. census takers were officially instructed not to record Poles as Poles (though some still did). In Minnesota, the large immigration from western Poland meant that many Poles who spoke fluent German were counted as Germans, especially in areas where Germans dominated the ranks of the census takers.

Close examination of samples from the 1905 Minnesota state census show that where Poles were counted as Poles, the census was fairly accurate. However, the census takers often missed entire communities, such as smaller groups of Poles residing in particular locales. In rural areas of the state, it is likely that between 25 and 30% of Poles were overlooked.

When census numbers are compared over time, significant discrepancies emerge. Between 1890 and 1905, for example, the number of foreign-born Poles grew to just over 300, despite large-scale immigration. Nor did reported census numbers square with the census calculation of the especially high birthrate among first-generation Polish immigrants. Between 1910 and 1920, the number of Polish speakers (both native and foreign born) increased only slightly despite the youth and high birth rate of the community.

In 1980 a new census category, "ancestry," allowed respondents to the long form to self-identify. Ten years later, 238,039 Minnesotans are estimated to have reported Polish ancestry, making Poles the state's seventh largest ethnic or racial group (sixth if French and French Canadian are counted separately). Although no figure is exact, given the demographic trends of the Polish American community, these figures seem to provide a reasonable estimate of the number of Poles in Minnesota.

Number of Poles in Minnesota: Official and Unofficial Estimates

	Foreign Born	Foreign Mixed	Foreign Stock	Mother Tongue	Ancestry
1860	127	21			
1880	2,267	1,189	(3,456)		
1890	7,503				
1905	7,881	19,337	(27,218)		
1910				49,120	
1920	18,537			49,490	
1930	15,015	33,896	(48,911)	13,265*	
1937			54,400		
1940	10,755			9,940*	
1950	8,392			5,358*	
1960			33,659		
1970	3,933	22,998	(26,931)	39,951	
1980					204,819
1990	2,331			5,755	238,039
2000	3,335			5,824	258,022

*Foreign born only

Polish Parishes in Minnesota

1   St. Stanislaw Kostka, Winona
2   St. Casimir, Winona
3   St. Casimir, Wells
4   St. John the Baptist, Minnesota Lake
5   Holy Family, East Chain Lake
6   St. Hyacinth, Owatonna
7   St. Joseph, Lexington
8   St. John Cantius, Wilno
9   Sts. Peter & Paul, Ivanhoe
10 Sts. Cyril & Methodius, Taunton
11 St. Adalbert, Silver Lake
12 St. John the Baptist, New Brighton
13 St. Mary, Czestochowa
14 St. Joseph, Delano
15 St. Adalbert, Albertville
16 St. Joseph, Holloway
17 Trinity Evangelical, Sauk Rapids
18 St. Lawrence, Duelm
19 St. John, Mayhew Lake

20 St. Adalbert, Gilman
21 Sacred Heart, Gilman
22 Sts. Peter & Paul, Gilman
23 St. Elizabeth, Alberta
24 St. John Cantius, St. Cloud
25 Immaculate Conception, St. Ann
26 St. Hedwig, Holdingford
27 O. L. of Mt. Carmel, Opole
28 St. Joseph, Ramey
29 St. Hedwig, Morrill
30 Holy Trinity, Royalton
31 Holy Cross, North Prairie
32 St. Edward, Elmdale
33 St. Stanislaus Kostka, Bowlus
34 St. Stanislaus, Sobieski
35 Holy Cross, Platte
36 St. Adalbert, Little Falls
37 O. L. of Lourdes, Little Falls
38 Sacred Heart, Flensburg

39 St. Joseph, Browerville
40 St. Isidore, Sturgeon Lake
41 St. Joseph, Split Rock
42 Sacred Heart, Silver
43 St. Casimir, Cloquet
44 O. L. Star of the Sea, Duluth
45 Sts. Peter & Paul, Duluth
46 St. Josephat, Duluth
47 St. Joseph, Gnesen
48 St. John the Baptist, Virginia
49 St. Joseph, Buyck
50 St. Stanislaus, Perham
51 St. Joseph, Oslo
52 St. Mary, Florian
53 Blessed Sacrament, Greenbush
54 St. Aloysius, Leo
55 St. John Sand, Caribou
56 St. Mary, Richardvill

the free-trade movement Solidarity in the early 1980s. Third, economic immigrants who arrived in the U.S. in the late 1980s and 1990s.

The early waves of Polish immigration to Minnesota came from a country that had lost its independence at the end of the 18th century and remained partitioned between Austria, Germany (Prussia before 1870), and Russia. Most of the immigrants began their lives as peasant farmers. Prior to the mid-19th century, these Poles were tied to the land and the landed nobility through a network of rights and obligations. With the advent of peasant emancipation, however, these obligations were often converted to cash rents, leaving the rural villagers with small pieces of land but with bills that had to be paid in cash. This sparked migration for wage labor—first locally and then of increasing duration and distance. Many Polish farm families supplemented their income with seasonal migrant labor, following harvests on the major estates of Prussia, Denmark, Sweden, and Russia. Other families, who saw little prospect of gaining their own land under these conditions, sought land in the New World: Brazil, Canada, and most of all the United States.[3]

A handful of Poles at most came to Minnesota during territorial times. These were most certainly political immigrants who had fled their homeland in the wake of the November Insurrection of 1830–1831 against Russian rule or the smaller revolts in the 1840s in Austria and Prussia.[4] Polish immigrants began to arrive in the state in appreciable numbers in the 1850s, primarily from the German-controlled western regions of Poland: Kashubia (Kaszubia), Pomerania, Poznania, and Silesia. These regions of Poland enjoyed a somewhat more prosperous and modern system of agriculture, and the people were more familiar with a cash-based economy. As a result, they were less inclined to associate farming with impoverishment and were more likely to be interested in once again taking up farming in the New World. Their fellow immigrants from the Austrian and Russian partitions were, by contrast, more attracted to wage labor in cities and mines. Generalizations, however, are hard to make since Poles from Austria and Russia settled on Minnesota farms, and many Poles from Germany could be found in cities.

Rural Settlement

By the start of World War I, Polish rural settlements existed throughout the state. Although nationally only about 10% of Poles settled in rural areas, by some estimates about a third of Minnesota Poles were living in farming communities. Polish immigrants established some 40 different communities in rural Minnesota, with another half dozen more in immediately adjacent areas of the eastern Dakotas. In Minnesota there were approximately 50 Roman Catholic parishes, five Polish National Catholic parishes and chapels, and at least one Missouri Synod Lutheran congregation where the population was either entirely Polish or where Poles constituted the vast majority of community members. Most of the rural settlers came from the German-ruled regions of western Poland, although there were a small number of Poles from Austrian Galicia as well. Poles from the Russian-held regions of Poland were the least likely to go into farming. The exception to this was the Polish community around Sturgeon Lake and a few scattered Poles from the east in Lexington, in central Le Sueur County.[5]

The first Polish settlement in Minnesota was the quasi-rural community of Kaszubs who settled around Winona by the late 1850s. Within a decade, the town was home to some 50 Polish families, and by the turn of the century, Winona had the largest single Polish community in the state, numbering about 5,000. Many probably migrated

Polish workers in a Winona lumber mill, 1890s. Poles worked in Minnesota's logging and timber industry throughout the state. It was common for boys as young as 12 or 13 to go to work to help support their families.

from other Kaszubian communities in Wisconsin, Michigan, and Ontario. These early pioneers worked in Winona's lumber mills—logging was a common profession in their home region near the Baltic Sea—and often maintained small farms on either the Minnesota or the Wisconsin side of the Mississippi River. Winona's Poles thus developed a kind of mixed economy with both wage labor and family farms.[6]

After the Civil War, more Poles came to take up farms in Minnesota, often following earlier German or Czech immigration patterns. In the 1860s Silesian immigrants began settling in Wright County, around the town of Delano. These immigrants spoke German as well as Polish and may have learned about Minnesota from German neighbors in the old country. The first Poles settled in Morrison County at about the same time. Polish immigrants also started to trickle into McLeod County where they settled alongside Czech immigrants in the Silver Lake area.[7] In the 1870s Kaszubs and Silesians established a series of small settlements in Walsh County in North Dakota, Opole in central Minnesota, Wells in Faribault County, in Edison Township in Swift County, New Brighton in Ramsey County, and Gnesen in St. Louis County, north of Duluth.

These early communities were formed by a process of chain migration in which the first arrivals gradually attracted their family and friends to the same area. For example, in 1888 the English-language newspaper in Royalton reported that "Merchants entertained 18 Polanders who arrived direct from the old country, 4 men and the rest women and children. They have relatives in North Prairie and intend to settle there." This type of immigration resulted in communities that grew slowly at first and only later became large enough to support institutions such as a parish church. Another feature of such settlements was their relative homogeneity. Kaszubs and Silesians seem to have been the most likely to form such communities and to have retained the strongest sense of regional identity. Winona, for example, was identified as a Kaszub community quite early on, due in no small part to the activities of the famous Kaszub writer and newspaper editor Hieronym Derdowski. Polish communities in New Brighton and Holloway, Minnesota, and in Day County, South Dakota, were also identified as Kaszubian.[8]

Silesian communities, such as Wells-Minnesota Lake, Delano, Opole, and Browerville, were also distinctive. The Wells Polish community originated from the area around a single village in Silesia, Syców. The Delano community retained a kind of mixed regional identity at least during its early years. Over time, its members seem to have adopted primary identities as either Polish or German. The first parish, St. Peter's, became mostly German speaking but was served for a while by a Polish priest, and the current church was designed by a Polish architect. In 1884, one group broke to form Polish-speaking St. Mary's in the hamlet of Czestochowa (a church designed by the same architect who designed "German" St. Peter's). Another group

St. Joseph's Church, built in 1908–09 in Browerville, is on the National Register of Historic Places.

of Polish speakers stayed with St. Peter's for two more decades, only breaking in 1904 to form St. Joseph. Members of all three parishes probably spoke the same basic Silesian dialect. It was not unknown in some Silesian families for one branch to consider itself Polish and another German.[9] Such distinct community histories could only exist in settlements created by chain migration from a single region of the old country.

At the same time, very different Polish rural communities were being created as planned colonies. A range of colonization efforts was carried out among Polish immigrants in the United States in the 1870s through the 1920s. They were initiated and fostered by railroads, the Catholic Church, and the two largest Polish-American organizations, the Polish Roman Catholic Union of America and the Polish National Alliance (PNA), both based in Chicago. The motivation for these colonies ranged from financial gain through land sales to a desire to save peasant immigrants from the moral and physical perils of life in the teeming industrial cities of the East and Midwest. Although the first attempts to form Polish farming colonies took place in Nebraska and Arkansas, efforts to settle Poles in Minnesota began as early as 1877. A report from that year states that a Polish association in Chicago—possibly the PNA—had purchased 25,000 acres of land in Benton County for a farming colony. Another report stated that the colony was being organized by one of the editors of the Chicago newspaper *Przyjaciel Ludu* (The People's Friend).[10] However it was formed, the colonization project does not seem to have been successful, and the newspaper itself folded by 1880. Yet, the area was already the focus of significant in-migration of Poles due to chain migration.

The clearest example of a planned farming colony is the Polish community in Lincoln County. With the cooperation of the Archdiocese of St. Paul and Minneapolis and the Winona and St. Peter Railroad, two Polish promot-

The Franciszek Otto family at their Lincoln County farm, about 1900

ers from Chicago, Antoni and Grzegorz Klupp, recruited Poles from Illinois, Pennsylvania, and Minnesota to settle around the new hamlet of Wilno beginning in 1882. The colony was promoted in the Klupps' newspaper, *Gazeta Chicagoska* (Chicago Gazette), and through agents who visited Polish immigrant communities. The effort was also backed by many of the leading figures in the Polish National Alliance, many of whom purchased land in the new community either as a speculative investment or with the intent of settling there personally. Within two years, some 450 Poles had moved to Lincoln County, and more had purchased land with the intent of settling there later. As a paying proposition the colony was doubtless a loss for the Klupp brothers, who passed from the scene rather quickly. Nevertheless, the colony itself proved both successful and durable.[11]

The Wilno colonists shared several key features. First and foremost, they were recruited from other Polish communities, primarily urban centers such as Chicago's near northwest side and La Salle, Illinois, rather than from the old country. Although 96% were born in western Poland, there was no single point of origin in Poland. Nevertheless, the colonists were demographically quite homogeneous. A sample of the original settlers showed that 43% were born between 1845 and 1850 and one-fifth were born in just two years, 1848 and 1849. Nearly all were married and had children. Most came to America between 1871 and 1881, with 46% arriving in the years 1879–81. Most worked in industrial wage jobs for a few years in American factories, quarries, or mines, and quite a few continued to work at these jobs for several years after they purchased their farms in Minnesota.[12] Unlike the settlements formed by chain migration, Polish colonies were made up of men and women who were already familiar with life in America and who had close connections and often relatives in major Polish centers such as Chicago. Because the colonists came in a large group within a few years of each other, they had the critical mass needed to establish parishes. Most colonization schemes were predicated on founding a Polish parish, which was seen as a necessary prerequisite for attracting Polish farmers.

Efforts to organize Polish farming colonies did not end with the Lincoln County community. The Censor of the PNA, Franciszek Gryglaszewski, was active in promoting several Polish colonies, including ones in northwestern Minnesota in Marshall, Roseau, and Kittson Counties. The towns of Florian, Leo, Hallock, Grygla (named for Gryglaszewski), and Stephen all developed small Polish communities in the 1890s. The great distance of these communities from major Polonia centers in the U.S. made it more practical for them to be served by Polish-speaking priests from Winnipeg. Another colony emerged around Sturgeon Lake in Pine and Carlton Counties. Although some chain-migration settlement occurred there, the St. Paul and Duluth Railroad promoted this colony heavily in Polish newspapers, such as Winona's *Wiarus* (The Faithful One).[13]

Most Polish immigrants learned about rural colonies and settlements by word of mouth from friends and family or from individual colonization agents who spoke Polish and sometimes took great pains to attract each individual. Companies and settlements also relied on ads in Polish newspapers to get the word out. Ads appeared in three different varieties. Larger companies and some communities commonly used display ads showing model farms. Short testimonials by satisfied colonists—which were misleadingly set to look like news stories—often accompanied these ads. Smaller Polish communities, from as far away as Idaho, relied on letters to the editor. Paweł Fajter, for example, wrote to *Wiarus* from Swift County, Minnesota, noting that the harvests that year had been excellent and

> The past year we built a church, but now it is already too small. If we get some more families we will have to build a new one. We have five good farms here, up to 160 acres,

Polish threshing crew in southwestern Minnesota, 1915. Many Polish farmers bought such equipment collectively to save money and avoid debt.

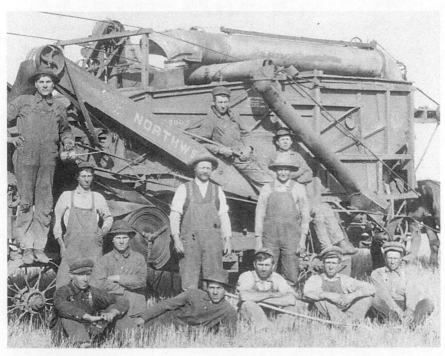

that are for sale, and so whoever wishes may buy, even on credit.

But they should hurry because these farms will be sold soon.

We wish that many Poles would take up farming, because to us the earth is like a mother.[14]

A group of Poles from Hallock wrote "each 160 acres of land has magnificent soil with beautiful [word missing] and the highest quality water. . . . We invite Polish people to come here and buy cheaper land. You better come now and not wait. Come, buy land and live here. After a few years you will be in a better situation than the people who live in the city and work in the factories and coal mines. If you want a better life come here."[15]

Some were less favorable to the whole idea of farming colonies. Some railroad officials and others considered Poles inferior, members of an alien race. For example, Charles Lamborn, the land commissioner of the Northern Pacific, wrote, "Do not send out any Polacks. There is a great prejudice against them. The M[innesota] and Manitoba people have refused to sell land for a colony of Polacks to settle on, as they claim they keep good settlers from coming in. A *few* stray Polacks, Chinese, or any thing else won't do any harm, but too many of a kind set down together in a new country will be detrimental." For the most part, however, railroad companies were in competition with one another for settlers and colonists and could not afford to indulge the prejudices of their officials or stockholders. Just a few years after Lamborn's remarks, the Northern Pacific was actively courting Polish colonists for its lands west of the Cascades in Washington State.[16]

Not all Minnesota colonization efforts were successful. A generation after the founding of the Lincoln County colony, a group of Poles from that community tried their hand at starting a new Polish colony in Aitkin County.

Their Nova Polska Company seemed promising enough on paper, but the poor soil of northern Minnesota and lack of interested buyers ended the effort prematurely. Other efforts were simply fraudulent. Two Polish promoters from Milwaukee tried to interest their countrymen in a variety of colony schemes in Morrison and Redwood Counties, even enticing them with dubious claims that the prospective farmland also had valuable minerals, such as coal. The pair was later arrested in Wisconsin for allegedly defrauding Polish immigrants in a similar land deal. Colony promoters in Minnesota also faced competition from other states. One notice in a Chicago newspaper called Minnesota "the American Siberia" and encouraged Poles to settle in Colorado instead.[17] By the 1900s, good farmland was harder to come by, and Poles from the Russian and Austrian partitions, where farming was associated with poverty, made up the bulk of new arrivals in America and Minnesota. These immigrants sought wage labor and looked to Minnesota's industrializing cities for homes and jobs.

Urban Settlement

The arrival of Poles in Minnesota's urban centers of St. Paul, Minneapolis, and Duluth, as well as in smaller towns with significant industry or mining such as Winona, Virginia, and Cloquet, dates to the 1870s. Prior to that, Poles were found in significant numbers only in Winona. Poles in St. Paul were at first widely scattered, often taking up residence in the least desirable areas, namely the "flats" along the banks of the Mississippi River.[18] They reaped the benefit of catching driftwood for home heating and an occasional fish for the dinner table, but their small homes were the victims of frequent floods.

St. Paul's Poles, most of whom initially came from the German partition, formed the first cohesive Polish community in the Twin Cities. In 1872, an estimated

70 Polish families combined with local Czech Catholics to form St. Stanislaus parish on West 7th Street. However, this parish became increasing Czech and after 1874 was served only by Czech priests. In 1878, the Poles began to separate themselves from St. Stanislaus, occasionally holding Mass in the basement of the cathedral when a Polish-speaking priest was available. In 1881, the Twin Cities' first Polish parish, St. Adalbert (parafia św. Wojciecha) was founded in the Frogtown neighborhood, an area then inhabited mostly by Germans, especially *Ostdeutsch* from east-central Europe and Austria.[19]

The choice of the Frogtown location was probably determined by the fact that an old church building from a French Canadian parish was available, as was inexpensive land. The 1885 state census shows relatively few Poles living in and around the parish; census takers even listed the Polish pastor as a German. At that time, outside of the river flats, most Poles in St. Paul lived in scattered clusters of a few families. The 1895 census, however, shows a major change—a large influx of Poles moving in from other areas of the city and new arrivals from Europe who together began to concentrate in the Frogtown area. Polish-owned shops, saloons, and organizations also appeared in the area. The Polish parish was the major attraction, but settlers were drawn to cheap land to buy or build houses as well. The many small factories and large rail yards nearby provided a ready source of employment.[20]

The early 1890s were probably the peak period for Polish arrivals in St. Paul. A large number found work on the city's industrializing East Side. In 1892, East Side Poles founded St. Casimir's parish (parafia św. Kazmierza). Although most of the parishioners were newly arrived from Poland, some moved in from the Frogtown area, either to get better jobs or to be closer to family. Poles also came to South St. Paul to work in the Union Stockyards after the turn of the century. Many may have migrated from Chicago, and by 1922 they numbered about 75 families.[21] This community remained without its own parish until 1941 when Holy Trinity was founded.

In the decades before World War II, the largest concentration of Polish-born St. Paulites was around the East Side community of St. Casimir with more than 6,000 foreign-born Poles. A large number of older Polish immigrants remained around St. Adalbert, but the community became increasing the home of the children of the initial immigrants, leavened by a steady influx of second-generation Polish Americans migrating from rural areas. Surprisingly, a significant number of Poles remained on the West Side of the Saintly City and in West St. Paul, with lesser numbers scattered in other areas of the city.[22]

Whereas Polish communities developed first in St. Paul, the largest and most recognized Polish concentration was in Northeast Minneapolis. A few Poles settled in Minneapolis by the early 1860s, and their numbers grew gradually until the 1880s when a large influx of Galicians from the Carpathian Mountains of southern Poland swelled the city's Polish community. As in St. Paul, the first Poles in Minneapolis settled along the flats of the Mississippi River. Most chose to live close to the lumber mills between Marshall Avenue and the Mississippi River and between Broadway to the north and Fifth Avenue to the south. Some found homes a little farther down river in the area below the Washington Avenue bridge known as Bohemian Flats. Many of the early arrivals resided among German immigrants, just as in St. Paul, and quite a few attended the German St. Boniface parish.[23]

The Galicians who settled Northeast Minneapolis came from what are today three areas: Polish, Slovak, and Rusin (or Ruthenian). At the time of immigration, they did not possess a strong sense of ethnic identity, and primary loyalties were to family, church, and village rather than to abstract concepts such as "nation" or "ethnic group." All

Nordeast

Northeast Minneapolis, known to some as "Nordeast," is the place in Minnesota most popularly identified with Poles. Other places might have larger, older, or more concentrated Polish communities, but in the minds of many, Nordeast was where the Poles lived. Giant, ornate churches and bars with names like Mayslack's and Stasiu's seemed to be everywhere. Northeast was to many the other side of the tracks. Nothing symbolized this better than when the city of Minneapolis dredged fashionable Lake of the Isles. It used the sludge to fill in Lake Sandy, Northeast's only lake. In an age of nativism, anti-Catholicism, and anti-Semitism, the area's ethnic difference was a source of embarrassment for city elites. While in a later age, other, newer immigrants would be embraced as part of the Twin Cities' diversity, the Poles and other immigrants who made up Northeast would never be so loved.

For the reform minded during the first half of the 20th century, Northeast was a "problem" to be solved. Its inhabitants were too foreign, too poor, too Catholic, and too out of touch with the "progressive" mainstream. For example, Northeast's women relied on midwives to help them in pregnancy rather than going to a hospital with modern facilities and staffed with male doctors. One social worker reported, "The Polish women are chief among our foreign born who rely upon midwives. It is therefore not surprising that in a survey of our City . . . it should be definitely found that in the North East there are a larger number of midwives than in any other section of the City." Many of the residents of Northeast lived in dire poverty even by the standards of the day, though many later reported that they did not feel poor because everyone they knew was the same way. One resident recalled, "My gosh we were poor. I didn't realize it at the time but I did as I got older."

Life in Northeast was defined by work. Men worked in flour mills that never stopped grinding grain and came home covered in flour, looking like ghosts. "Pa would carry deadheads back from the river on his back," the son of one immigrant remembered. "Deadheads were logs that had been en route down the river from northern Minnesota and had gotten waterlogged and never made it to the mill. . . . They were very, very heavy. He dried them out and we used them for firewood for heat or cooking."

For those who came from Northeast, though, their home turf was a source of fierce if often wounded pride. Yet it was also a place where its residents felt safe and at home. Neighbors knew each other and spoke the same languages. You could start a story in Polish and finish in English and everyone would know exactly what you meant. As one resident remembered, when the local bands practiced their polkas and obereks, the local children danced in the streets. And then there were sports teams. Ethnic Northeast took to American sports because it offered a level playing field and chance to succeed where the rules were clear and you were judged by your ability rather than your accent or your last name.

The homes were, for the most part, simple and inexpensive but well maintained. The paychecks from a lifetime of grinding toil were invested in those homes. Outsiders might sneer at the seeming obsession with property values that people in neighborhoods like Northeast seemed to have, but few understood that the homes were nest eggs against bad times, the only legacy they would be able to pass on to their children. To lower one's property value was to lessen the value of a lifetime of hard labor and tight budgets. In the 1990s, as older residents died off, these same homes began to attract a new generation of blue-collar immigrants, this time from Mexico and south Texas. So the soil in which the dreams of one immigrant generation took root was made fertile for the next generation of newcomers.

spoke mutually intelligible mountain dialects. As the largest and best organized group, the Poles, led by a few more ethnically conscious immigrants from western Poland, were the first to form a parish, Holy Cross parish (parafia św. Krzyża) in 1886.[24] As a result it was the Poles, more than any other group, that would have the most influence on the development and character of Northeast. At the time, a significant number of Slovak and Rusin Galicians attended Holy Cross, and even after the formation of separate ethnic parishes for these groups, a sizable number of Polonized Rusins and Slovaks remained at Holy Cross.

The Biennas family, who came from what is now Slovakia, was one example of this phenomenon. Anna Biennas recalled that "I attended Holy Cross school until the eighth grade. When I went to kindergarten I didn't know English. . . . When we had lived in Czechoslovakia [sic], we spoke Hungarian because of the Austrian-Hungarian [sic] government. But when we came to America my father insisted that we learn English, and we said our prayers in Polish. It was hard to keep the three languages straight." Far from being a separate group, these Polonized Galicians seem to have integrated seamlessly into the Polish community.[25]

As Minneapolis's milling and brewing industries expanded, more and more Poles flocked to Northeast and North Minneapolis. This soon necessitated the founding of additional parishes, as Holy Cross grew unable to handle the growing population. In 1906, St. Philip (parafia św. Filipa) was founded in North Minneapolis. This was followed by St. Hedwig (parafia św. Jadwigi) in 1914, situated north of Holy Cross on the east side of the river, and All Saints (parafia Wszystkich Świętych), located south of Holy Cross, in 1916.[26] Although Galicians still came in large numbers, after 1900 Poles from the Russian partition of Poland were an increasingly important segment of the new population.

Polish settlement in Duluth—along with the establishment of a Polish community in next-door Superior,

Wisconsin—forms a separate chapter of the history of Minnesota Polonia. Poles initially came to Duluth to work in the city's lumber mills and docks. By 1876, at least 30 Polish families were living in Duluth, enough to form a separate Polish church society. This led to the creation of the city's first Polish parish in 1881, Our Lady Star of the Sea (parafia Matka Boska Gwiazda Morza). A directory of the parish published a decade later indicated that the overwhelming majority of its members were simple laborers (84% of 253 male parishioners). Duluth's second Polish parish, Sts. Peter and Paul (parafia ŚŚ. Piotra i Pawela), was founded in 1901 on the West End. Poles also settled in other small industrial and mining towns of the north. In Cloquet, they came for jobs in the local paper and sawmills.

The F. L. Meehan Tailor shop in Virginia with the Polish-born proprietor and two of his young Polish women employees

Polish immigrants in front of their home in Finn Town,
a neighborhood in Virginia, 1900

Although Poles worked throughout the Iron Range and in
winter logging camps, the largest permanent Polish concentration on the Mesabi Range was at Virginia. Poles on
the range seem to have originated from the Russian partition, especially from the Łomża region and the Rajgród
forest. In Virginia these immigrants worshipped at the parish of St. John the Baptist, which was predominantly Polish
but also served some Slovaks and Slovenes. Even farther
north was the tiny Polish community at Buyck, which
mixed farming, trapping, and logging.[27]

Family, Home, and Parish

Although the exact number of Poles in Minnesota at one given time during the early years of settlement is difficult to ascertain given available data, what is clear is that the state's Polish communities grew rapidly. The expansion of urban communities between 1890 and 1914 caused by new immigration was only part of the picture. The biggest population increases were among the children of these immigrants. Poles in Minnesota had extraordinarily high birth rates. A study of the 1900 census, undertaken for a congressional inquiry into contemporary immigration, discovered that in both urban and rural settings Polish women were having larger families than any other ethnic or racial group. In a survey of 21 Minnesota rural counties, the study found that over 70% of first- and second-generation Polish women had given birth to more than five children. (In the next highest group, "Russians," the same number stood at 62%.)[28]

The result of this was very young communities. In Lincoln County, more than half of all Poles were under the age of 16 in 1905. In urban areas, families tended to be slightly smaller; nevertheless in St. Paul in 1900, 48% of Poles in the Frogtown area were under age 16. These numbers more than offset the high child mortality rates suffered by the Poles.[29]

Large families were the result of a culture that valued and cherished children, but also served a practical purpose. In rural areas, children's labor provided an important supplement for pioneer families. What set Poles apart was that women as well as men worked outdoors and in the fields, a fact that often disturbed Anglo observers. One noted, "The Polish farmer gets out of debt by employing hand labor ... [substituting] muscular and family labor for capital and equipment." Children who reached the age of 15 or 16 sometimes got wage jobs of their own, working as do-

Mrs. Frank
Ochocki and five
of her children at
work in the family
garden near
Hendricks

mestics in cities and towns or as farmhands in rural areas.
Some Polish young people from rural Minnesota traveled
as far as the Twin Cities or Chicago to work during part
of the year. In 1893, Kazimierz Pawlak returned to Lincoln
County from Chicago "where he was staying during the
winter, and brought back a great pile of money."[30]

The use of family labor had economic advantages but
also created problems with local authorities and tensions
within the family. In some localities, Polish parents were
fined for not sending their children to school. There were
also cases of young people rebelling against parental au-
thority, especially by running away from home. In most
instances, however, it was difficult for young immigrants
to succeed on their own without the emotional and financial support of families. The importance of intact family
units and the primacy of the family over the individual was
further reinforced by the practice of arranged marriages,
which were not uncommon in some communities prior to
World War I.[31]

For Poles, as for most ethnic groups, the home and the

Polish farm family in southwestern Minnesota with horse-drawn reaper. Unlike some immigrant groups, in Polish families women and children participated in all aspects of farm and fieldwork.

family were the center of life. Yet, establishing or reestablishing homes in the New World in the absence of a village of extended family members and familiar places and customs was difficult and often painful. Married couples with children frequently arrived in Minnesota with very different expectations that had to be reconciled with the reality of pioneer life. When Jakub Górecki brought his wife Róża to their new home on the prairies of western Minnesota, her response to his imagined dream farm was less than enthusiastic. Raised in a close-knit village of family and neighbors near Poznań, Róża Górecka, like so many pioneer women, had to adjust to life in a sod shanty on the open prairie. "Oh Jakub," she exclaimed on first seeing her new home, "you've cast us out on the wind."[32]

Aside from the hardship posed by the elements, it was,

perhaps, the cultural and social aspects of family life that immigrants missed the most. Polish women in Minnesota had to create homes and families without the help of mothers, grandmothers, and aunts. This gave them more freedom on the one hand, but also much greater burdens on the other. It demanded flexibility and creativity in responding to the challenges of preparing children for life in a world they themselves did not fully understand. One scholar wrote, "More and more immigrant mothers came to depend on friends, neighbors, and outsiders for support. . . . In the absence of the usual support network of female relatives, the women had to expect more help, support, and companionship from their daughters and their husbands than was customary."[33]

Family networks were stretched thin by the trans-Atlantic migration and by the need to find security in America. Polish immigrant families were far more mobile than is commonly believed. Poles in rural communities not only moved to greener pastures in newly established colonies elsewhere, but also traveled back and forth to visit scattered relatives in Chicago, the Twin Cities, or other places. The same means of modern transportation that helped pull families apart could help them to reconnect. Many Minnesota Polish farm families paid yearly visits to their urban relatives or hosted their city cousins during the summer. Rural families got a chance to earn money or partake of new cultural experiences while their urban counterparts escaped the city and returned with fresh produce, even carrying crates of live ducks and geese back with them on the train. Poles in urban settings could also be very mobile, both in terms of residence and in seeking out better jobs. A study of first-generation Poles in St. Paul found that about a third of the families surveyed changed either their place of residence or the job of the head of head of household every five years.[34] As always, the goal of such movement was to improve the economic situation of the family. To this end,

A group of Lincoln County Poles on vacation at Fish Lake, South Dakota, about 1900. The parish priest, Fr. Józef Cieminski, sits at lower left. This group brought fishing poles, a shotgun for birds, a cookstove, and other refreshments (note the beer tap and whiskey bottle on the wagon in the background).

the desires of individual members often had to be sacrificed for the betterment of the family as a whole.

Polish immigrant families in Minnesota lived lives of change and flux, and this sometimes had a bad effect on parent-child relations. Rural and urban communities were often the scenes of disorder. A correspondent from St. Paul complained to *Wiarus* of young Polish women "dancing in a saloon with some fellows. . . . When it was already midnight I was awakened by this whirling and I heard such shrieks in the street and noise that I thought the neighbor's house was on fire. . . . One should not be surprised at the young ladies who do this, but we should deplore the mothers whose daughters knock about the streets in the dark of night, becoming the laughingstock of other peoples." Mirroring more recent immigrant groups, a 1926 study of juvenile delinquency in St. Paul found that Poles were over-represented in juvenile crime statistics. Young Polish women who worked in restaurants were perceived by both community leaders and outside social workers as being under a special threat; the critics often viewed this type of work as a form of "white slavery." Rural communities, too, faced significant social problems.[35]

Although these problems affected only a portion of the Polish community, the rapid changes that immigrant families faced made such situations seem all the more threatening. To counter the perception of instability in their own lives and to anchor themselves more firmly in their new Minnesota homes, Poles invested their hearts and souls in their most significant community institution—the parish. More than almost any other ethnic group, Poles made the parish the center of their lives, and it was the parish that provided a sense of stability and permanence in a world of change.

Parish and Community

Nowhere was the intersection of the private life of the family and the public life of the community more evident than in the ritual life of the parish. Although Polish immigrants came to America with a rich tradition of cultural and religious ceremonies, they tailored them to fit their new lives in Minnesota, adding and subtracting elements in ways that could be both planned and spontaneous. Yearly church rites provided a ready-made set of community events and celebrations, giving the Poles a sense of continuity in a world of change. The midnight Christmas Eve Mass at St. Casimir's in Cloquet, for example, was typical of the elaborate rituals beloved by Polish immigrants: "About a dozen or more altar boys with their red and white vestments and high celluloid collars and gold braid would help serve Mass. The altar would be jammed with lighted trees

Symphonies of Stone and Stained Glass

When Polish immigrants came to Minnesota, the first and most important community institution they created was the parish. As one scholar noted, for Poles in America, "churches stood as visible reminders that God had come with the immigrants on their long journey and that perhaps the voyage had been worth it. They were stone and mortar roots which bound them to the soul of the new world. . . . Few peoples have ever had as great a sense of place and of history as have the Poles and because of it they are determined to hang onto their beloved churches."

Polish church buildings became the visible expressions of the community. Its members had little money or influence, and they were at the bottom of Minnesota's social ladder. The Poles did not see themselves as poor and lowly, but as people possessing a story, a deep faith, and an innate dignity. With few artistic outlets available to them as working-class people, they channeled their hopes, dreams, and ambitions into the building of magnificent churches that expressed their new identity as Polish Americans. In Europe, only the nobility and the rich built churches, but now, in America, the sons and daughters of humble villagers who had grown up in thatched-roof huts were the ones contracting with architects and commissioning bells and stained-glass windows.

Polish churches and those of their central and eastern European neighbors differed markedly from those built by immigrants from northern and western Europe, both Protestant and Catholic, stemming from different concepts of God. For the Polish immigrants, God was not distant and aloof, but present in the world around them. As scholar Dennis Kolinski wrote, "Traditional Slavic consciousness saw the realm of the sacred as the whole world around us. The sacred permeated the entire landscape." Thus the churches built by Poles in Minnesota were rich in decoration, color, and movement, often in the neo-Gothic or neo-Romanesque style with flourishes of Baroque and Rococo and the more contemporary Beaux Arts styles. Many churches also incorporated Polish national symbols into their decoration and design, such as the crowned eagles or rose windows

St. Stanislaus Catholic Church, Winona, Minnesota, completed in 1895 was a landmark for the city's Polish community.

St. Casimir Catholic Church in St. Paul, 1925. The parish church was designed by émigré architect Wiktor Kordela who designed many churches for Polish and east-central European immigrants in Minnesota and Wisconsin.

with the symbols of the old Polish Commonwealth—the White Eagle of Poland, the Horseman of Lithuania, and the Archangel Michael of Ukraine. At St. John Cantius in Wilno, an unknown local sculptor, in crafting panels of the four Evangelists for the pulpit, portrayed St. Mark dressed as the Polish-American hero Thaddeus Kościuszko.

The first church built by the Poles of Lincoln County in the 1880s was merely a timber frame covered with shiplap that shifted in the winter wind. But soon, the community pooled its resources, and by 1901 it built a towering brick church, filled with stained-glass windows. Its twin steeples were so tall that on a clear day they could be seen as far away as Marshall, 20 miles to the east. In Winona, the Poles stunned their neighbors by building the huge, domed church of Stanislaus Kostka that towered over the tiny workers' cottages of the Polish neighborhood. (Such impudence could not be forgotten, and when Winona became the seat of its own diocese, this magnificent church was not chosen as the cathedral in preference for a smaller but non-Polish church.)

One of the most prolific church architects in Minnesota was Wiktor Kordela. Born in Kraków of a mixed Polish-Italian family and educated in the multicultural, multireligious city of Lwów (Lviv), Kordela came to America in the 1890s and by 1902 became a partner in a Minneapolis architectural firm. His most frequent commissions came from Polish communities in Minnesota and Wisconsin. He designed St. Casimir in St. Paul, St. Mary of Czestochowa near Delano, Our Lady of Lourdes in Little Falls, and St. Joseph in Browerville. One of his last commissions was for the new parish church of Holy Cross in Minneapolis in 1927.

The churches built by Poles helped to humanize and sanctify the visible landscape, making a notable impact on skylines and cultures both urban and rural. Although the descendants of Polish immigrants have largely remained loyal to the parishes built by their forebears, others have been less respectful. After Vatican II, some misguided Catholic Church reformers sought to purge parishes of what they considered old-fashioned styles, and the intense Old World piety of Polish culture was high on their target list. In Winona, the magnificent St. Stanislaus Kostka was gutted, its statues and pulpit sent to the trash heap. Some courageous parishioners managed to save these items, created through such sacrifice by their parents and grandparents. The church's statues and pulpit panels remained in private hands until the 1990s when a more sympathetic pastor refurbished the church for its centennial.

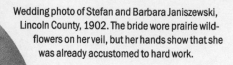

Wedding photo of Stefan and Barbara Janiszewski, Lincoln County, 1902. The bride wore prairie wild-flowers on her veil, but her hands show that she was already accustomed to hard work.

and the manger scene. Long before midnight there would be standing room only in St. Casimir's. About 11:30 P.M., the organ would start playing, accompanied by violins.... The choir ... would literally make the rafters ring with their rendition of 'Dzisiaj Betlejem.'"[36]

Weddings were equally elaborate. One account from Sobieski in central Minnesota noted that the festivities began when the best man, "sometimes clothed in a uniform and upon a regal horse, would stop at each home and in a clear voice recite by rote a lengthy invitation address in Polish rhetoric." The wedding usually lasted for two or more days:

A great selection of food was laid out, including innumerable pastries. Music and dancing were the mainstays. Young men were encouraged to dance with [the] bride only after they had offered a small monetary gift in exchange. A plate was set out for the men to deposit their payment for the pleasure of the dance. The coin was thrown violently onto the plate in hopes that it would break. If it did break and was not replaced or a metal one was set out to take its place, the prospective dancers would drift away.... The festivities would occasionally end at the end of the second day. The next Sunday an extension of the celebration took place. The participants may have been fewer but the leftovers ... were enough to carry the party on for some time.[37]

Observances of important feast days like Corpus Christi could be just as dramatic. Altars were set up a mile from the church in each of the cardinal directions and the entire community processed from one to another. At each one, the priest said Mass and read from one of the four gospels. In Wilno in 1893, the procession consisted of, first, all the school children, then the Rosary society, the Society of St. Michał, six altar boys, twenty girls dressed in white, the priest Fr. August Zalewski, the choir, and finally the rest of the parishioners.[38]

One key characteristic of Polish immigrant rituals was the lack of separation between participants and spectators. The entire community participated. In every celebration or event, each family, organization, and group was at least symbolically represented: men and women, lay and clergy, children and adults. Disunion in the form of political or personal conflicts that kept community members from rejoicing together was long remembered as a stain on the community's good name.

Although processions for religious holidays like Corpus Christi could be found in many immigrant communities,

St. Stanislaus Catholic Church, Sobieski

Poles also created their own tailor-made rituals. In 1893, the Wilno community marked its first silver wedding anniversary, that of Michał and Magdalena Tykwiński. Such anniversaries would not have been commemorated in Poland, but this one was nothing like the wedding anniversaries celebrated in the U.S. either. It was, instead, a completely new creation and as such was carefully planned in advance by the pastor and some of the leading men and women.

The festivities began on a Wednesday afternoon in early January. With St. Michał's Society leading Mr. Tykwiński and the women's Rosary society leading Mrs. Tykwińska, the party went in procession to the church carrying banners and candles. Waiting for them at the church door was a large group of parishioners. As the couple approached the church door, these parishioners pulled out rifles and revolvers and began firing into the air with a sound like "the broadside of a battleship." Before the gunshots had died away, the bells started to ring and the choir began singing "Veni Creator," creating a tapestry of sound and texture.[39]

The first death that occurred after the Wilno Poles arrived "out on the wind," as Róża Górecka had put it, was an occasion not only to mourn the deceased, but also to reflect on being buried in an alien land, far from the graves of friends and relatives. The funeral of Anna Felcyn (who died leaving several small children) in 1886 featured a procession with 30 wagons. Beginning at her home at 8 A.M. and proceeding past nearly every farm in the community, the procession lasted for six hours before reaching the church. Everyone stopped work for the entire day to attend

Interior of St. John Cantius Church, Wilno, decorated for Easter, about 1900

the funeral Mass. A final procession to the cemetery—nothing more than a plot of land set in the vastness of the wind-swept prairie—ended in a graveside sermon by the pastor that was so emotional that all present—men, women, and children—were moved to tears.[40]

The intense emotion of such scenes was a common feature of Polish community life, especially when the immigrants were reminded of their homeland and the relatives they had left behind. In 1886, St. Adalbert parish in St. Paul was the scene of the first Mass of a newly ordained priest, Fr. Jakub Wójcik, as a correspondent for *Wiarus* described:

At 10 A.M. our pastor, Fr. D[ominik]. Majer, together with other priestly ministers and led by the Holy Cross, went in procession from the church to the rectory whence they led the newly made priest to the church. Then, Holy Mass began, celebrated by Fr. Wójcik.... During Holy Mass Fr. D. Majer gave the homily and it was so moving that nearly everyone wept uncontrollably. He spoke about the dignity of chaplain and also how fortunate were the families who could see their sons as priest and be present at their first Holy Masses. But alas! The family of the newly ordained priest could not enjoy this good fortune because God had ordained that they be separated by many thousands of miles. Here in this land of America he would celebrate his first Holy Mass, but thankfully it would be among Poles who could at least in part replace his mother and father and thus, as Fr. D. Majer said, offer prayers so the Lord God would give him strength and comfort in His Holy Grace on the thorny path that priests must trudge.[41]

A group of first- and second- generation Poles socializing at the parish rectory, Wilno, about 1910

The rituals and celebrations centered around the parish were not only religious in nature. Patriotism for a Poland

whose independence had been lost before any of the immigrants had been born was also a vital way to build community out of the disparate elements in each enclave.

On November 30, 1892, Wawrzyn Pawlak wrote to the Polish newspaper in Winona to describe one such occasion in the Polish farming community of Silver Lake, a holiday to celebrate the November Insurrection of 1830–1831 against Russian rule in Poland:

> We wish to inform you that we commemorated the anniversary of the November Uprising.... Never before had so many people arrived to any such celebration.... Our big basement was literally crammed with men and women. This shows that patriotic feelings are on the rise every year.... Every member of our military forces came to the commemoration and in full dress marched from the hall to the church and back again. After singing the national anthem, our most reverend pastor, Fr. Tyszkiewicz opened the celebrations. In his speech, he presented three types of heroes of the November Uprising: the peasant, the townsman, and the nobleman. The pictures he painted with words were so moving that we had to wipe away our tears every few minutes.... Mr. Pauszek spoke next about how we, Poles in America, should celebrate the memory of all the heroes of the November Uprising, not only on this one day, but with continuous work.... His speech was interrupted with continuous applause.

After the speeches, a group of schoolgirls, many with tears in their eyes, recited patriotic poems, so that "one could see their sincerity, that they understood what they said." Following a series of patriotic songs, the pastor took the floor again to assure the audience that the dead heroes of 1830 were grateful for their prayers. "We, exiled from our homeland, are united with those who passed on, and with those who remain in Poland; there is no power that can

National Holidays

Polish immigrants had, for the first time in their lives, a chance to celebrate Polish national holidays. Political conditions in the homeland, economic hardship, and lack of education often restricted Poles' ability to celebrate key dates in Polish history. In their new homes, however, they were given both the freedom and the time to keep these holidays.

Nevertheless, the immigrants had few models on how to observe important national days, so they adapted American models from celebrations of Memorial Day or the Fourth of July. The models they chose were very much in keeping with the spirit of late 19th-century middle-class America, combining self-education, moral exhortation, declamations of poetry, and musical interludes. They kept minutes of their celebrations and wrote detailed reports of their events and proudly sent them to Polish American newspapers. In some cases, Polish immigrants completely took over American holidays. In Lincoln County, Poles turned the Fourth of July into a completely Polish-speaking event.

The most important and durable Polish holiday is May 3, Polish Constitution Day, which marks the adoption in 1792 of the world's second democratic constitution (after the United States). The constitution was also an effort at national revival that was quashed by Poland's powerful neighbors. Despite this, the ideals of the constitution and the moral courage of its drafters inspired subsequent generations of Poles to dream of freedom and democratic self-rule. In Minnesota, the first May 3 celebrations were held by the 1870s, if not sooner. Subsequent generations of

May 3 parade at the Polish American Club in St. Paul, 1976

Polish children in historical and folk dress appealed for donations in St. Paul, 1917.

immigrants and their descendants have come together ever since to mark the day. The oldest continuous celebration in Minnesota is undoubtedly at Holy Cross parish in Minneapolis, where May 3 is celebrated by recent Polish immigrants in much the same manner as when the parish was founded in 1886.

Of nearly equal importance to the first wave of Polish immigrants was November 29, a holiday that commemorated the start of the November Insurrection of 1830–1831 when a group of young officers of the Russian-controlled Polish army began an ill-fated attempt to overthrow tsarist control and establish an independent state. More than any single historical event, this lost cause fired the imagination of Poles in the diaspora. January 22, the start of the 1863 uprising in Poland, was also remembered but less commonly than November 29.

Poles in Minnesota and across the United States largely overlooked Poland's Golden Age during the Renaissance when the nation's borders stretched from the Baltic Sea to the Black Sea, when art, learning, and culture flourished. Instead, they found their inspiration in the tragic era of the partitions and in the heroic struggle of small bands of patriots facing the overwhelming might of Imperial Russia. "Suffering Poland" became an idea fixed in the minds of Polish immigrants, many of whom came to see their own leaving and the separation from friends and family as part of Poland's larger tragedy, even though few were forced to emigrate for political reasons.

When Poland regained its independence in 1918, commemorations of the tragedies of the partition era became less common. In Minnesota, celebrations of November 29 died out by the 1930s in most places. Pulaski Day, October 11, was observed by some Polish organizations, though never as enthusiastically as in cities like Chicago and New York.

Poland's new independence day, November 11, which coincided with Armistice Day, did not catch on until after World War II (ironically, after Poland had again lost her independence). This holiday came to America with postwar immigrants who grew up with Independence Day celebrations in Poland and was reinforced by subsequent waves of immigrants in the 1980s and 1990s.

sever these bonds of love. An enemy can take our land and fetter our bodies, but there is no force that can enslave our national spirit." The celebration ended with everyone singing "Bożę coś Polskę" (God Save Poland).[42]

Polish immigrants in Minnesota, as elsewhere, invested much time and effort in creating and sustaining their community life. The Polish hamlet of Silver Lake, for example, had three military units with historic dress. One was a cavalry company. Another dressed as scythemen in honor of the famous unit of peasants who charged the Russian artillery under the leadership of Tadeusz Kościuszko at the epic battle of Racławice in 1794.[43]

Being the focus of so much community interest and involvement also made parishes the cockpit for the most intense conflicts both within and outside the Polish community. Priests, as leaders of the parish, were either revered or reviled. The parish of St. John Cantius in Wilno had a series of problems with the powerful archbishop of St. Paul, John Ireland, who sought to purge immigrants of their culture as fast as possible. In 1897, the parish's new priest, Fr. Apolonius Tyszka, arrived from Illinois but was immediately the subject of a series of poison-pen letters to Archbishop Ireland from some enemies in his former parish. Eighty-eight members of the Wilno parish sent a letter of protest to *Wiarus*:

> Some subverters in the Polish parish in La Salle, Ill., people without faith, conscience, shame, or honor, enemies of the Holy Church and of priests, cover us all with shame and disgrace, by causing discord and quarrels in our Polish parish in Wilno, Minn. These messengers of hell write letters against our parish priest, Fr. A. Tyszka. . . . They are real Judases, enemies of Christ and friends of the devil, envying us the peace we have, the peace they themselves have lacked for many years. Therefore, at a parish meeting on February 2, 1897, we, members of the Polish

parish in Wilno, disgusted to the highest degree by the maliciousness and calumnies of some of the hooligans in La Salle directed against our parish priest, resolved publicly to protest against them as enemies of God's cause. We declare that we have nothing to do with them and that we do not believe them at all. . . . We express our regrets, because many people in La Salle suffer from these malicious, abject, and ignoble Herods and Pilates. We tell you, vile Catholics and Poles, that your letters will not be of any help to you—they are a waste of time, ink, and paper, because we do not have such disturbances here. We work hand in hand and if there is a Judas among us, he has already received his reward.[44]

Despite the support of the parish, Ireland immediately removed the popular Fr. Tyszka from his post, sparking further protest. The parishioners sent a delegation to Ireland, who reportedly received them coldly, calling them rebellious vagabonds and mocking them by stating that Poland had deserved to lose its independence and be torn apart by its neighbors. To add insult to injury, Ireland then appointed a Czech priest to take Fr. Tyszka's place. This caused some of the Wilno parishioners to consider breaking away from Ireland's control and forming an independent parish, but Fr. Tyszka demurred and remained obedient to the archbishop.[45]

While the Wilno parishioners remained in the church, some Poles elsewhere did leave their churches. These splits were rarely over doctrinal issues, but rather over parish control. In 1907 a group of Poles in Duluth formed St. Josephat, the first Minnesota parish of the independent Polish National Catholic Church (PNCC). In Minneapolis, several families from Holy Cross broke with that parish in 1914 to found Sacred Heart of Jesus Polish National Catholic Church after they had an argument with the pastor. A number of local disputes among Poles in Morrison and Benton

Counties led to the creation of two independent churches, neither of which was large enough to support permanent pastors, though they survived for several decades as missions of the PNCC. Overall, the PNCC probably never claimed more than 1,200 members in Minnesota.[46]

The attitude of many of Minnesota's Catholic bishops toward their seemingly quarrelsome Polish flocks was dismissive. Archbishop Ireland even was alleged to have suggested that Polish divisiveness would result in Congress expelling Poles from the U.S., though the bishops granted that as long as Poles fought over their faith they were not in danger of losing it. The major exception to this attitude was Bishop James Trobec of St. Cloud whose Slovenian heritage and knowledge of basic Polish gave him better insight into his Polish flock than most of his fellow bishops. In April 1912, he issued a unique pastoral letter to his Polish parishes to address their spiritual and administrative problems. It is the only known example of such a letter issued by an American bishop during this era of serious unrest in Polish American parishes.[47]

Despite the problems inside parishes that upset the harmony the society sought and that seemed all too common to contemporaries, the Polish American parish community worked well overall. Among the first generation of pastors, only a few such as Fr. Majer of St. Paul were able to hold both the trust of their bishop and the loyalty of their parishioners. After the turn of the century, however, pastorates in Minnesota's Polish parishes grew more stable as more and more American-born clergy came to the fore. They were familiar with the American Catholic Church and its Irish-dominated hierarchy and had the ethnic consciousness to minister to the cultural and spiritual needs of their flocks. Many would become not only community leaders but would also play a major role in shaping and mobilizing ethnic consciousness on behalf of their communities and the Polish homeland.

After the pastor, the most important part of the parish community was the school and its teachers. Polish immigrants put a high premium on building and sustaining parochial schools that taught faith and morals and well as Polish language, history, and culture with a further dose of American history and basic English. The earliest schools were staffed by lay teachers, often men who doubled as the church organist. This proved less than satisfactory. Pay was poor, and it was often impossible to retain teachers. The community news columns of *Wiarus* show that turnover among early lay teachers was high. Other teachers were less than qualified. One "Professor" Marcin Kurek served several Minnesota parish schools for short stints. The parishioners of Wilno fired Kurek "on the grounds of intemperance and as unqualified for the position he held."[48]

The solution to the problem of teachers was women religious from teaching orders such as the Sisters of St. Felix, School Sisters of Notre Dame, or the Franciscans

Beginners' class ("Początkowa Klasa") from St. Stanislaus parochial school, Winona

of Rochester. In the latter order, founded by German and Luxembourg women, a quarter of all sisters were Polish by 1907. Service in these orders was an attractive option for young Polish women who sought education and career paths other than that of wife and mother. As teaching sisters, they represented a tremendous mobilization of talent on behalf of their young communities, and they came to wield major influence and shape the character of their parishes.[49]

Schoolchildren playing tug-of-war outside their parochial school, Wilno, 1930s

The parish provided a home for many other institutions. Among the most important were religious societies, such as women's rosary societies and men's clubs. These groups had important religious and social purposes but also served a self-help function. They provided crucial opportunities for leadership as well. In order to maximize leadership positions, Polish communities tended to develop new groups rather than increase the size of existing ones. The result was a proliferation of parish organizations, many of which were connected to larger fraternal societies. In 1920 in Duluth, for example, Poles were second only to the Swedes in the numbers of ethnic associations despite their relatively small population.[50]

Parish organizations were run on a democratic basis and taught democratic political behavior. They took obvious pride in writing careful and detailed constitutions and in legally registering their societies with civil authorities. They often published their constitutions in the Polish press. Such societies also enforced moral standards and taught a code of conduct that emphasized fidelity and personal responsibility. The St. Anthony of Padua Society at Holy Cross provides an example of a typical parish society:

Membership was limited to Polish Catholics of good physical and mental health between the ages of eighteen and thirty-five. Its object was mutual Christian help in sickness and misfortune, and members were charged with the duties of visiting the sick, burying the dead, and helping widows. Its banner bore the face of St. Anthony on one side and the picture of a sick person receiving Holy Communion on the other. The society's insignia was a wide red and white band that was worn over the left shoulder, across the back and breast, and joined at the right hip. Its orchestra wore red and blue. The members received Holy Communion twice a year, at Easter and on their patronal feast.

A candidate for membership was introduced to the society by a member, after physical examination by a doctor had indicated that he was eligible for membership. Two members were appointed to investigate the candidate's reputation. If the investigation was favorable ... he was brought before the president to be questioned about his age, his practice of religion, his familiarity with the society's constitution and his willingness to abide by it, and about membership in any forbidden society [e.g., the Masons]. Then the membership voted to accept or reject the candidate. Seven ballots against meant a rejection.

Five ballots against postponed the vote.... If only four ballots were voted against the proposed candidate he was accepted. All opposing votes had to be accompanied by written reasons for opposition.... The organization had an elaborate system of fines ... to improve discipline. Fifty cents was charged for forgetting one's emblem, ten cents for using tobacco at a meeting, a dollar fine for the first time a member was intoxicated at a meeting, a two dollar fine for the second occurrence, and ejection at a third occurrence.

The entrance fee was four dollars and yearly dues were three dollars. The sick benefit was four dollars per week after the first week.

Another Polish church society in rural Minnesota stipulated that it would not pay death benefits for a member who died under immoral circumstances.[51]

Community and Organizations

Although usually based in the parish, lay organizations transcended parish boundaries and gave the local Poles a window on the larger Polish community in the United States and its politics. The most important associations in this respect were the local units of the major and competing Polish fraternal benefit societies, the Polish Roman Catholic Union of America (PRCUA) and the Polish National Alliance (PNA). While many began as independent parish societies, the benefits of joining these national federations quickly attracted most local groups into their folds.

The struggle between the PRCUA and the PNA had deep roots in Polish and Polish American history. Both sought to unify the immigrant community under their respective banners and each had its own concept of what the community ought to be and do. Although the major conflicts occurred in Chicago (where both were headquartered) and other large centers in the East and Midwest, in the 1880s, the growth of Minnesota's Polonia gave it early political clout and a role in shaping the course of the struggle.

At the center of these conflicts was the patriarch of Poles in the Twin Cities, Fr. Dominik Majer. Fr. Majer had been a founding member of the PRCUA but had a sharp disagreement with that organization's dominant leader, Fr. Wincenty Barzyński of Chicago. Fr. Majer then participated in the PNA, which claimed to be the standard bearer of Polishness in America. In the mid-1880s, he led a group of priests, mainly

Fr. Dominik Majer, the patriarch of Poles in St. Paul and founder of the Polish Union of America

from Minnesota and Wisconsin, who threw their support behind the secular PNA. Their public declaration that the PNA was fully compatible with Catholic ideals undercut the message of the rival PRCUA, which asserted that it was the voice of Catholic loyalty among Polish immigrants. Fr. Majer and his "Alliance priests" group, along with PNA Censor Franciszek Gryglaszewski of Minneapolis, attracted the national convention of the PNA in 1887 to St. Paul. Through Fr. Majer's good offices, the convention was even addressed by Archbishop Ireland in his only known speech to a Polish audience. This honeymoon, however, did not last long. Although the PNA was deeply focused on the cause of Poland, anti-clerical elements had a strong voice. In 1889, these forces drove Fr. Majer and most of the Alliance priests out of the PNA.

Some of Fr. Majer's colleagues rejoined the PRCUA, but the St. Paul pastor had other ideas. In 1890 he formed

Blessing of the banners of St. Joseph's Society, No. 893 of the Polish Roman Catholic Union of America, St. Casimir Catholic Church, St. Paul, June 1918

his own fraternal federation, the Unia Polska (or Polish Union), based in St. Paul. His goal was for Unia Polska to be the middle ground between the Catholic PRCUA and the secular PNA, drawing members from both and bringing about the elusive goal of unity among Polish Americans. By 1900 Unia Polska had 109 societies nationwide. In Minnesota, it had 10 societies, compared to 13 for the PNA, and only one for the PRCUA. Its official newspaper *Słonce* (The Sun) was also based in St. Paul. Despite this temporary success, however, Unia Polska failed to bring unity to Polonia. In 1901 it moved its headquarters and newspaper to Buffalo, and before World War I internal divisions caused it to split into three separate factions.[52]

Although the two main fraternal organizations presented clear ideological contrasts, on the local level such distinctions had little impact on membership. Individual immigrants joined one group or another because family, friends, or coworkers were members. By World War I, most Twin Cities parishes played host to members of both societies, and it was not uncommon for one person to be a member of both fraternals. The largest of these societies rarely numbered more than 200, but their multitude made up for the small size of individual groups. Some smaller federations also existed, such as the Polish Roman Catholic Union of Winona. A more significant group was Polish White Eagle Association (PWEA), founded in 1906 in Minneapolis probably by dissident members of the PNA. Unlike the PNA, members of PWEA had to be Roman Catholics in good standing. This was similar to several other PNA breakaway groups that split from the parent organization over ideology.[53]

Although the larger ideological battles between the big fraternals were rarely relevant to Poles in Minnesota, local conflicts between the rivals were sharpened and driven by personal disputes and dislikes. When Fr. Majer and Unia Polska members did not participate in the May 3 celebrations in 1898, local PNA members publicly accused the St.

A society picnic for members of the Polish White Eagle Association Group 15 featured a beer-drinking contest, about 1930.

The Polish American Press in Minnesota

One of the most important elements binding any modern community together is its media. The first Polish immigrants in the state had no newspaper and thus relied on Polish newspapers from Chicago, Detroit, Wisconsin, New York, and Missouri, which were probably read in the state by the late 1870s and 1880s. In the mid-1880s, only the Polish community of Winona had the critical mass of subscribers to sustain a local press. In 1886, Fr. Romauld Byżewski founded the newspaper *Wiarus* (Faithful One) in the southeastern Minnesota town.

Fr. Byżewski hired activist and writer Hieronym Derdowski as his editor, but within a few years Derdowski took over sole proprietorship. Derdowski was already well known as a poet and polemicist in Poland and served brief stints with other Polish newspapers in the U.S. Derdowski's works in the Kaszub dialect had made him the unofficial poet laureate of the Baltic Coast region from whence he came. Yet, it was his polemics that garnered him the most attention. Derdowski attacked the leadership of both major factions in American Polonia, earning him the ire of many, and both secular and religious opponents at times sought to stop fellow Poles from reading his publication. At the same time, Derdowski's newspaper provided a forum for Poles in many small communities, like Silver Lake or Puck, South Dakota, to send in reports of local activities that otherwise would never have found a venue.

In the late 1880s and early 1890s, *Wiarus* was one of the most widely read Polish newspapers west of the Mississippi, reaching into Wisconsin, Texas, Nebraska, and the Dakotas, as well as many eastern states. The growing number and diversity of Polish newspapers in the late 1890s cut into *Wiarus*'s standing, and Derdowski's death in 1902 put an end to the newspaper's national prominence. It remained popular in Minnesota and the Dakotas under the editorship of his widow until it was taken over by *Nowiny Minnesockie* in 1919.

Nowiny Minnesockie (Minnesota News) was a business venture developed in 1915 by a group of St. Paul businessmen who capitalized on the growing population of Polish Americans who were never attracted to the more-established *Wiarus*. Most of its readers lived in the Twin Cities and central Minnesota. *Nowiny Minnesockie* held the record as the state's longest running and most stable Polish newspaper, existing under the editorship of one man, John Koleski, from its founding until it ceased publication in 1978. It was undeniably a success, but its editor's refusal to adapt to the reality of an increasingly English-speaking community ensured its ultimate demise.

Minnesota Polonia created other publications that were more ephemeral. Many parishes published bulletins in Polish that included local news items and devotional pieces. A short-lived effort

Paul priest of holding the community back out of egotism. On the other hand, a local ally of Fr. Majer derided the program speakers at a PNA-sponsored celebration: "Next was a lecture by Mr. Rakowski, as long as a Chinese opera, boring the good listeners who applauded with joy because it was over." Hieronym Derdowski, the maverick editor of Winona's *Wiarus*, made a career of irritating all sides. In 1889, several St. Paul Poles complained about the "gypsy editor" (*cygański redaktor od Wiarus*) and his newspaper,

Mr. and Mrs. Hieronym Derdowski on their wedding day

to establish an English-language newspaper by the publishers of *Nowiny Minnesockie* seems to have produced only a few issues in the early 1940s, perhaps falling prey to wartime economic strictures.

Poles in Minnesota also avidly read newspapers from other Polish centers in the U.S., though evidence about them is spotty. The major fraternal publications, mainly based in Chicago, had a significant readership in Minnesota. The newspapers *Rolnik* (The Farmer) and *Gwiazda Polarna* (the North Star) from Stevens Point, Wisconsin, and other Badger-state periodicals such as *Kuryer Polski* (the Polish Courier from Milwaukee) had a Minnesota readership. A wide variety of Catholic religious publications circulated in the state, often produced at the Polish Seminary in Orchard Lake, Michigan, or the Polish Franciscan center in Pulaski, Wisconsin. *Straż* from Scranton, Pennsylvania, was read by local adherents of the PNCC. Poles also read their local English-language press, and in areas with large Polish communities, the local English newspapers ran occasional items in Polish.

In the early 1980s, activist and community leader Czesław Róg founded the English-language newsletter *Pol-Am,* which has filled a gap caused by the demise of *Nowiny Minnesockie.* It is frequently sent at the editor's expense to local Polish-American parishes, prominent Polish leaders, and others. Originally a mimeographed sheet, it has since become a professionally produced periodical and even has a readership outside of Minnesota. Others have appeared on the scene, including an informative and professional-looking newsletter for Polish-American genealogists and one for Polish Kaszubs. In addition, the revitalization of the Polish-language ministry at Holy Cross parish has resulted in a monthly Polish-language bulletin, which has varied in format and content over the years. Poles continue to subscribe to out-of-state publications, including *Polish American Journal* (Buffalo) and *Polish News* (Chicago), both of which feature occasional Minnesota news items.

which they described with the English-loan word "garbage." At least two merchants announced they would boycott Derdowski's newspaper "Because H. Derdowski ... unfairly besmirched the name of citizen Langowski and did so only to bring sorrow to a Pole who for the sake of our dear country endured exile in Siberia."[54] These disputes, however, remained largely among community leaders who were usually clergy and small businessmen, often saloonkeepers.

Other more specialized organizations emerged to fill gaps that the fraternal societies could not cover. Republican and Democratic clubs promoted citizenship, voting, and support of Polish candidates for local elections. A Polish-American Building and Loan Society helped immigrants in St. Paul and Minneapolis to own their first homes. In rural areas, Polish farmers formed agricultural circles that shared farming techniques and township fire insurance companies, such as the Sobieski Mutual Fire Insurance Company in Wilno.[55]

Another community institution was less formal but no less important: the saloon. A largely male establishment, the saloon served immigrant workers as a social club and place to get a cheap meal, which was especially important for single men and married men whose families remained in Poland. Although frequently criticized by social reformers and many clergy for promoting drinking, saloons and their owners were centers of political organizing and community building. Some saloonkeepers parlayed their trade into other businesses. Stanisław Kozlak of Minneapolis helped his fellow Galician immigrants with immigration matters, arranging money transfers and steamship tickets. Józef Matz of St. Paul became a liquor wholesaler and held stock in a variety of other Polish-run businesses, including the newspaper *Nowiny Minnesockie* (Minnesota News) that he helped found in 1917.[56]

Fraternal societies were a major means to mobilize the community, and in the period before the development of Polish cultural organizations, social clubs, and folk dance groups, they were also the earliest promoters of Polish American culture. Prior to Polish independence and with immigrants having differing customs and dialects and coming from different regions of Poland, this cultural activity played a vital role in making a cohesive Polish community. The most important activities were community-wide celebrations in which the societies played a key role,

Saloon in Wilno, about 1900. On Sunday afternoons, following Mass and devotions, men gathered for a glass of beer and to socialize.

but they also sponsored their own activities. Among the most notable was the development of Polish library societies and theatrical groups.

Groups like the Enlightenment Society, later known as the Kościuszko Society, promoted amateur theatrical and literary events. By World War I, virtually every Polish school and parish of any size in Minnesota had an amateur theater group. Libraries were also significant. The Union of Lublin Library Society in St. Paul, founded in 1893, promoted "learning among Polish youth through reading good and useful books." By the turn of the century, its library had nearly 250 volumes as well as periodicals and brochures. It also sold classics of Polish literature at reduced prices to members. Women's membership was encouraged with discounted admission fees. "Thus," one description stated, "one should not wait but should join and avail oneself of

Fr. Franciszek Rakowski and a children's theatrical group dressed in homemade Polish costumes, Wilno, Minnesota, about 1917

the knowledge-filled books in the library." A similar library, sponsored by the PNA in Northeast Minneapolis, was founded about the same time.[57]

The Cause of Poland and the World Outside

National consciousness grew quickly in Minnesota Polonia in the 1890s and early 1900s. It was hastened by the American setting, which helped transform the immigrants' ideas of who they were. Faced with people from many different cultures, Poles sought to define who they were and what it meant to be Polish in the American context. Ironically, the first step toward becoming more American was to become more ethnically Polish. Coming from villages where education had been limited and where expressions of Polishness were discouraged or banned by the authorities, immigrants in America began to learn about the culture and history of the land they had left behind. They listened to the music of Chopin, heard the poetry of Mickiewicz, and read the novels of Sienkiewicz. In so doing, they encountered what has so often been the central obsession of Poles in the diaspora—the cause of Polish independence. After 1900, as the international political situation changed and Polish groups in the United States became better organized and more sophisticated, efforts to aid the struggling homeland became both more urgent and more effective.

Early efforts to help Poland were focused on collecting money to aid victims of repression or building up the National Fund created by exiles in Switzerland. A pastor or a fraternal society usually organized these efforts. The turning point came during the height of German and Russian repression in the first decade of the 20th century when Poles from across the country began to mobilize to bring the Polish cause to the attention of the American public. In 1908, a series of German land expropriations aimed at reducing the Polish presence in Western Poland brought 1,000 Poles to the rotunda of the Minnesota State Capitol in protest. They delivered a resolution to the legislature "calling on all civilized nations, in particular the United States, to protest against these wrongs." Poles from St. Cloud drafted letters to President Theodore Roosevelt and Representative C. A. Lindbergh, exhorting them to protest to the German government.[58]

This campaign had some success, and for the first time, the press in the Twin Cities began to report on Polish issues, and American politicians began to pay at least lip service to the desires of Polish voters. In 1909 the *Minneapolis Journal* opined that "even today, partitioned and held down, Poland triumphs in the mind and rich temperament of her children who are the superiors of their stupid Russian conquerors."[59]

These efforts, as basic as they might be, signaled that Poles in the North Star State were increasing comfortable protesting as Americans, using American methods and ideas of freedom and justice. They also indicated a growing internal consensus on the need to help Poland. By 1912 Poles nationwide were putting aside their internal bickering and taking the first steps toward forming a national umbrella association. In that year, the Komitet Obrony Nardowy (KON or National Defense Committee) was formed, and a Minnesota section seems to have been active by 1913. KON, however, was dominated by socialists, and the major Polonia organizations soon defected. By 1915 the Polish Central Relief Committee was established and took most of the mainstream locals with it, including what had been the Minnesota branch of KON.[60]

During World War I and the subsequent Polish-Soviet War (1919–22), Poles in Minnesota flexed their new organizational muscles on behalf of Poland. Fighting on the Eastern Front raged across Polish lands from August 1914 onward, causing massive destruction and loss of life and creating millions of refugees. Outbreaks of famine and disease soon followed, and the American press reported extensively on "starving Poland." This, in turn, brought local relief efforts to the sympathetic ear of Anglo-Protestant society and clubwomen, such as Mrs. Sumner T. McKnight, who otherwise would have had little to do with Poles. In May 1915, with the support of these activist Anglo women, a group of young Polish women, dressed in Polish folk costumes, set up collection boxes in prominent downtown Minneapolis locations, including Dayton's, the Shubert Theatre, and the Scandinavian-American Bank. Many of the young women had relatives in Poland, and heartbreaking letters from suffering family members appeared in the newspapers as an added incentive for compassionate Minnesotans to donate. The drive netted over $850.[61] This effort was spearheaded and managed by a group of highly motivated and articulate young women who provided a photogenic, English-speaking face for Minnesota's Polish community.

In 1917 the Allies allowed the creation of a Polish army, recruited from Poles living in the United States and trained in Canada. As the U.S. went to war in April 1917, Polish

Margaret and Leona Roszak and Stella Roszak Czechowicz were among the young second-generation Polish women who raised money for the Polish cause among Americans.

Americans, who were exempt from the U.S. army draft due to citizenship or language barriers, could enlist in this new fighting force. In Minnesota recruiting centers sprang up in Minneapolis, St. Paul, Duluth-Superior, and possibly Winona. The total number of Minnesota men who volunteered for or actually served in what became known as the "Blue" or "Haller" Army is unknown, but a preliminary survey of volunteers from northern Minnesota revealed nearly 450 names, indicating a massive response to the appeal.[62]

The Americanization campaigns of the World War I era

Recruiting center for the Polish Army, Minneapolis, about 1918

did not affect the state's Polish Americans as they did German Americans. Poles in Minnesota and elsewhere fused Polish and American patriotism into an almost seamless whole. Abraham Lincoln and George Washington were placed alongside Tadeusz Kościuszko and Kazimierz Pułaski as Polish American heroes. During the war, service to America was emphasized, and Poles sought to outpace other ethnic groups in the purchase of war bonds. One observer stated, "It was commonly remarked by the solicitors that the Polish people rarely refused to buy a bond." The problems that did occur as a result of Americanization tended to be in public schools where the occasional unsympathetic teacher simply treated all "foreign" students with the same contempt.[63]

Following the reestablishment of Polish independence in November 1918, Minnesota Poles shifted their focus to providing aid to Poland as it fought to keep its freedom in the face of hostile neighbors and a humanitarian catastrophe. Impoverished Polish communities across the U.S. struggled to meet a $10 million goal for Poland after years of frantic appeals and on top of the continuing needs of the

Polish army, Polish hunger relief, and the demands of their own relatives both in Europe and the U.S. Fund-raising went on throughout Minnesota. Poles in Lincoln County contributed more than $5,500 in 1919. Silesian Polish communities in the state not only provided funds but also staged public demonstrations in favor of including their home province within the borders of the new Poland. In 1918 the parishioners of Holy Cross sent over $2,500 to the collection point in Chicago and added further donations in the months that followed. Polish communities held ice cream socials and packed boxes of presents and newspapers for Polish soldiers. Some receipt book entries note the arrival of jars of pennies and nickels collected by Polish schoolchildren.[64]

The Interwar Period and World War II

Aided by the Polish diaspora, Poland was able to repel a major Communist invasion in 1920 and retained its independence. Yet for many Polish Americans the new Polish state was not the ideal they had imagined. Many who visited Poland realized that their time in America had changed them, and it was impossible to go back. In Poland, they were treated as Americans, while in America with nativism on the rise, they were treated as Poles and foreigners. In addition, a massive baby boom began to influence the community. At Holy Cross, baptisms peaked between 1912 and 1916, creating especially large parochial school classes and huge numbers of American-born young people in the 1920s and 1930s.[65] Their outlook and understanding of Polishness differed markedly from that of their parents.

The changing relationship to Poland and the growth of the American-born second generation caused Poles in Minnesota and elsewhere to look inward. Efforts to focus on so-called national goals articulated by some community leaders were largely ignored by the majority of Polish

Americans who did not feel a need to shop only in Polish-owned stores or speak Polish exclusively. The concerns of the local community became paramount, and the needs of Poland and attempts to establish a national Polish lobby became less important. At the national level, the wartime plan to create a unifying Polonia organization fell apart. Minnesota, however, bucked this national trend. The Minnesota Polish National Department remained active and in 1932 changed its name to the Polish Centralia, which remained in existence into the 1970s. The Centralia consisted of most of the Twin Cities Polish fraternal societies, as well as some local all-Polish chapters of groups like the American Legion, augmented by a few groups from outstate Minnesota.[66]

Another important organization that appeared during this period was the Polanie Club. The club, founded in 1927, probably emerged out of the activities of PNA group 1530, Gwiazda Wolności (Star of Freedom), a Minneapolis women's fraternal society. Many had played a role in the wartime relief work. The Star of Freedom group was active in promoting Polish cultural activities and the role of women in the Polish community in the early 1920s. Members of Polanie Club were American born or had immigrated as children. They were younger, married women and most were educated and equally comfortable in Polish and English.[67]

Polanie Club consciously embodied a Polish American identity and sought to develop and promote a Polish American culture based on folk art and music. Members reinforced this mission with trips to Poland where they collected examples of folk art, especially from the mountain regions of southern Poland. In addition, members such as Wiktoria Janda and Monika Krawczyk were creative artists in their own right and wrote poetry and short stories on Polish and Polish American subjects for English-speaking readers. Beginning in the 1940s, Polanie undertook an ambitious publishing operation aimed at English-speaking Polish Americans. In addition to the poetry of Janda, the club published

Stan Wasie: Pioneer of Overnight Shipping

In 1906 Stanisław Wasielewski arrived in Minnesota with his parents and settled in Northeast Minneapolis. Stanisław's mother, Franciszka, died a few years later, and by the age of 13 the boy was separated from his father and alone in the world. For the next few years, he was taken in by a Czech Catholic farm family in Scott County. By the time

Stan Wasie at the wheel of one of the trucks in his fleet

of World War I, he had returned to the city and went to work for Minneapolis Steel Machine. After the war, he got a job as a clerk and dispatcher for a trucking firm, Pratts Express, and married Marie Manikowski, the daughter of Polish immigrants living in Northeast Minneapolis.

In the early 1920s, railroads still dominated intercity shipping, but a few companies began to find a niche in short-haul transportation. This was the business the young immigrant learned. Where the hardships of his childhood might have sent another person into a tailspin, they showed him that to overcome he had to be a quick study and work twice as hard as the next guy. He shortened his name to Stan Wasie and rolled up his sleeves.

In 1927, Wasie started his own company, Merchants Motor Freight, Inc., with a single truck and an office in Northeast Minneapolis. The firm handled local transport and carried freight between Minneapolis and St. Paul but soon added other locations, including Rochester (with its expanding Mayo Clinic), Chicago, Des Moines, Kansas City, Detroit, Cleveland, Denver, and St. Louis. By the 1950s, the company had 800 vehicles and its own terminals and employees in half a dozen midwestern cities.

Wasie was one of the earliest to offer direct city-to-city overnight shipping. Merchants was among the first companies to employ automation in its terminals with conveyor belts, pneumatic tubes to deliver paperwork, computers to process freight bills, and radio-equipped trucks. One of Wasie's greatest innovations was the creation of a transport paperwork clearinghouse that streamlined and simplified the billing process, especially for smaller carriers. He was a founding member of several trucking industry associations and was the first president of the Middle West Motor Freight Traffic Bureau and served as vice president of the American Trucking Association. He was also the first president of National Trailer Pool, Inc., and pioneered the cooperative equipment pool for the trucking industry.

After selling his company in 1960, Wasie remained active in the community and in business. He established scholarships for young Polish Americans from Northeast Minneapolis and other Polish communities, especially for young men from working-class families. "I'm proud I grew up on the East Side," he once told a reporter. "Those kids over there don't have the same chance [as wealthier groups]. If I can help their situation a little bit, I'll be happy. . . . Poles are the hardest working of all the races." Wasie and his wife were supporters of the Como Zoo, the Boys Club, and the Sheriff's Youth Ranch. He bought a 680-acre farm in Scott County and used it to raise rare birds and deer as well as farm animals.

In 1966 Stan and Marie Wasie created The Wasie Foundation to continue offering scholarships to Polish American youth and to provide for other charitable activities. Through the foundation, the Wasies became the largest single donor ever to Abbott-Northwestern Hospital. Stan Wasie died in 1974, and Marie in 1992. The foundation they started still follows their original vision.

Color guard from American Legion Gopher Post 440 at the 32nd convention of the Polish National Alliance, Minneapolis, September 1955

a cookbook, a book of translated Polish songs, and works on Polish Christmas customs (to name a few). This was the first effort to codify markers of Polish American ethnicity and articulate Polish folk art and cooking for an American audience. The Polanie cookbook has gone through multiple printings, becoming the best-selling Polish cookbook in America with more than 100,000 copies in print by 2004.

Other organizations also emerged during this era. Among them were the Polish-American Club of St. Paul, the Winona Athletic Club, the Minneapolis Commercial Club, and the PNA Home Association and largely Polish sections of groups such as the American Legion. These groups emphasized building social ties and community service rather than overarching national or ethnic goals.

The changing nature of Polish American ethnicity was also demonstrated by a change in community activities. The emotional celebrations of the first generation that centered around the tragedies of Poland's long 19th century and the painful separation from home and family began to fade away. Celebrations of the November and January Uprisings continued on and off into the 1930s, with the last recorded commemorations occurring in Duluth in the mid-1930s. In their place, new heroes emerged. Pulaski Day, October 11, became more important and allowed Polish Americans to express their ethnicity and stress Polish contributions to America. Because a significant number of veterans of the Haller Army were Minnesotans, its former commander, General Józef Haller made two trips to the state during nationwide tours of the United States. In both instances, he received an enthusiastic welcome, as did other notable Polish leaders.[68]

Poland did not disappear as a wellspring of ethnic identity. Many young Polish Americans, usually from middle-class backgrounds, had new opportunities to visit Poland through programs such as those sponsored by the Kosciuszko Foundation. Nevertheless, "American" activities like baseball, basketball, or polka music played an ever-greater role in the community's social life. These American activities, however, were carried out largely within the Polish community. Sports was often the major exception (though here the context was often intra-Catholic sports leagues), since it provided a venue in which Polish American youth

The Polish New World Dance Group performed at the St. Paul Festival of Nations, 1936.

could compete on a relatively even playing field without fear of being shunned or discriminated against. The Polish community remained within its own ethnic boundaries. It was rare for young people to date across ethnic lines. As one man remembered, "If we dated somebody from the South Side a lot of times you'd hear 'You dating that Polack from Northeast again?'"[69] Both urban and rural parishes and their schools remained almost exclusively Polish American into the 1960s if not later.

The Second World War, which began with the invasion of Poland by Nazi Germany and its Soviet ally in September 1939, resulted in a major change in the sense of isolation and focus on internal affairs of Polonia, both in Minnesota and elsewhere. Once again, the needs of the homeland overwhelmed almost all other concerns of the community. Shock and outrage soon gave way to calls for humanitarian aid for the victims of Nazi and Soviet barbarity and for revenge against the hated invaders. The community threw itself into collecting money and supplies for Polish relief and to support the Polish armed forces that had reconstituted themselves in England to carry on the fight against

Polish National Alliance baseball team, Winona, 1939

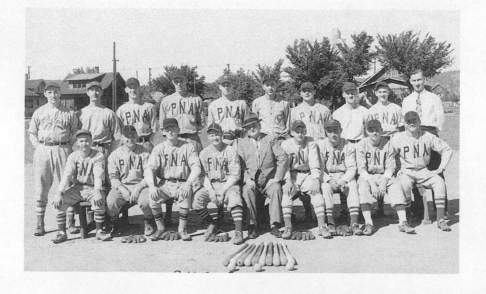

Hitler.[70] While many Americans remained isolationist, Poles strongly supported President Franklin Roosevelt's efforts to aid the Allied cause. During these years, local Poles were outspoken in bringing Poland's plight to the attention of their fellow citizens. Wiktoria Janda wrote some of her most impassioned poetry during this period, such as "In This Dark Hour," which was read locally and reprinted frequently. They also established a short-lived English-language newspaper, *The Polish American,* to appeal to English speakers inside and outside the community.

After the attack on Pearl Harbor, the war came home to Poles in Minnesota in an even more personal way. Due to the demography of the Polish immigration, many communities, especially in urban areas and on the Iron Range, had large numbers of young men of draft age. As a result, some parishes sent a huge proportion of their youth to fight the Axis. At St. John the Baptist parish in Virginia, nearly a third of the entire community had joined the armed forces by early 1944. At St. Stanislaus in Perham, one in five parish members wore the American uniform. In older, rural parishes the numbers were not as great. Poles nationwide served their country at rates slightly above the national average of the U.S. population as a whole.[71]

Minnesota Polonia after World War II

The war had several important effects on Poles in Minnesota and elsewhere and refocused much of the community's energy on the homeland and its plight. With Poland under the control of Soviet dictator Josef Stalin, Polish Americans took a keen interest in the Cold War and strongly opposed appeasing the Soviet tyrant, although their support for the Democratic Party remained solid. In addition, the community mobilized to lobby the state's congressional delegation and educate fellow citizens on behalf of Poland. In 1944 national Polonia groups had put aside differences and come together to form the Polish American Congress (PAC). In Minnesota, the Polish Centralia proved the ideal vehicle for such organizing and developed one of the charter state chapters of the PAC.

The war's social impact on Polonia was more complex. Many of Minnesota's young Polish Americans who had served their country in such numbers had formative experiences outside their community, parish, and family. Their new familiarity with the world beyond the ethnic neighbor-

Military Service in Selected Polish-American Roman Catholic Parishes, Minnesota, Spring 1944[72]					
Parish	Place	Membership	Members in Service	Deaths	Pct. in Service
St. Stanislaus	Bowlus	475	50	2	10.5
St. Joseph	Browerville	937	117	1	12.4
St. Casimir	Cloquet	450	61	1	13.5
Sts. Peter & Paul	Duluth	1,012	159	2	15.7
Sts. Peter & Paul	Gilman	1,350	114	1	8.4
St. Hedwig	Holdingford	458	79	2	17.2
St. Joseph	Kettle River	165	24	0	14.5
O. L. of Lourdes	Little Falls	990	104	2	10.5
St. Adalbert	Little Falls	450	63	0	14.0
All Saints	Minneapolis	1,800	275	3	15.2
Holy Cross	Minneapolis	4,100	578	6	14.0
St. Mary	Opole	546	65	0	11.9
St. Stanislaus	Perham	300	62	3	20.6
St. Adalbert	Silver Lake	892	75	0	8.4
St. Stanislaus	Sobieski	600	96	3	16
Holy Trinity	S. St. Paul	800	70	1	8.75
St. Adalbert	St. Paul	1,879	153	3	8.1
St. Casimir	St. Paul	2,160	314	6	14.5
St. John the Baptist	Virginia	654	192	2	29.3
Nativity	Willow River	160	17	0	10.6
St. John Cantius	Wilno	730	52	0	7.1
St. Casimir	Winona	600	112	2	18.6
Total		21,508	2,882	40	13.3

hood increased, prejudice lessened, and new economic opportunities beckoned. Although college education was still out of the reach of too many, after the war it seemed increasingly possible for Poles to make it in the mainstream society. For some of those who returned to rural communities after having traveled around the world and seen the carnage of war, the transition back to home life was just too much. One woman from Lincoln County remembered how her brother came back after the war and paced the floor at night "like an animal in a cage." Soon he moved to Chicago to start a new life. Others suffered from what they had seen and experienced, including many who had been victimized by Nazi tyranny either as civilians or as prisoners of war.[73]

At the same time, in the early 1950s a new group of Polish immigrants began to arrive in Minnesota. Some of these people had been enslaved as forced laborers in Germany or had been imprisoned in infamous Nazi concentration camps such as Dachau or Auschwitz. Others had survived Stalin's gulags and escaped in 1942 to India or the Middle East where many joined the Polish Army Second Corps that fought with distinction against the Nazis in Italy. Virtually all had suffered almost unimaginable horrors and tragedies. Some arrived to join distant relatives in Minnesota, others came on their own, resettling through aid agencies or migrating in search of a new life. At least one small group that settled in the Duluth area came from the Polish minority in Bosnia.[74]

The wartime experiences of these refugees had seared into them a strong national consciousness and a fierce opposition to the Communist takeover of their country. Their sense of Polishness and even their style of spoken Polish had been developed in Europe and was quite different from the language and culture of their American-born cousins. The immigrants saw the Polish Americans as too Americanized, insufficiently aware of modern Polish culture, and unmotivated by the pressing demands of the homeland. The Polish Americans viewed the new arrivals as arrogant, ignorant of the problems Poles faced in America, and ungrateful for the resettlement help they had received. The result was often friction and misunderstanding. At the same time, the newcomers injected fresh life into community affairs. They developed new fraternal societies. They and their children were instrumental in developing the state's first permanent Polish folk dance group, Dolina Polish Dancers, founded in 1949.[75]

Although nearly all of these new arrivals joined Polish parishes and most initially settled in old Polish neighborhoods, they were not wedded to these areas. The advent of the automobile allowed immigrants and second-generation Polish Americans alike to maintain their membership in ethnic parishes even if they moved elsewhere. In the 1960s and 1970s a steady trickle of Poles left Northeast for new suburbs such as Fridley and Columbia Heights. The Poles in North Minneapolis also dispersed, some following their Jewish neighbors who moved to western suburbs like St. Louis Park. Frogtown's Poles continued to own local stores and businesses into the early 1980s.[76] The East Side of St. Paul and Northeast Minneapolis remained heavily Polish American, but the tendency toward fewer extended families living under the same roof and greater geographic dispersion was evident everywhere. Leaving the old neighborhood did not always mean loss of community ties, and in some cases, new groups formed that maintained or strengthened ethnic identity.

The Polish language remained largely the language of the home and church, although it could still be heard frequently on the streets and in stores in Polish neighborhoods and small towns into the 1960s and 1970s. This Polish was often heavily Anglicized and in some ways became a dialect, but it was nevertheless recognizable to native speakers (if not always appreciated by them). The close tie between religious observance and language is illustrated

Dolina Polish
Dancers at the St.
Paul Festival of
Nations, 1958

by the case of St. Casimir's parish in Wells, where Polish was used regularly by parishioners until 1946 when a tornado destroyed the church. With parish life disrupted for several years during the rebuilding, customary gatherings and observances at which Polish was the primary language did not take place or were undertaken at other locations. Although the community recovered, use of Polish did not. In parish parochial schools, Polish-language courses were phased out by the mid-1950s, often at the insistence of parents who feared that retention of Polish would harm their children's economic prospects. Polish remained as a foreign-language course in some schools, including Edison High School in Northeast, into the early 1970s.[77]

The 1970s represented a kind of watershed for Poles in Minnesota. On one hand, the old generation was dying off, and use of Polish declined to the point where the state's only Polish newspaper, *Nowiny Minnesockie*, went out of business in 1972. The old Centralia and the state's chapter of the Polish American Congress fell apart during this era as well. Nationally, the entertainment industry and media singled out Polish Americans for stigmatization, and stores across Minnesota carried bigoted "Polish joke" products

At the Table with Poles in Minnesota

In 1990, when the Polish American Cultural Institute of Minnesota sponsored its first Polish Soup Fest, it was an acknowledgment of the role that food has played in binding together Polish American families and communities. This might seem strange in a state that has never had a Polish restaurant remain in business for long. Polish food has been mostly an affair of the home.

The early Polish immigrants brought an array of hearty dishes. Soup was a major part of every meal, and varieties were almost endless. The best known was red barszcz (borscht), a beet soup that could be served in almost stewlike form with lots of meat and vegetables or as an elegant clear broth on Christmas Eve, accompanied only by small mushroom-filled dumplings. Other common soups ranged from simple potato soup to the more exotic żurek (sour rye soup).

Coming from a background where meat was a luxury, Polish immigrants tended to consider it a necessity. A turn-of-the-century study of immigrants showed that Poles were the group most likely to spend disposable income on food. One Polish immigrant woman remarked, "Polish women feed their men more meat than do other women. . . . English [i.e., American] women buy less meat and more pies and pastries," but she allowed that "their men seem healthy enough nevertheless."

Both rural and urban families kept animals for their own table, but town dwellers often relied on rural relatives for this. Hogs were the least expensive and most commonly kept animal, and after the first hard freeze, Polish families usually slaughtered a pig for the winter, using the entire animal. Also pork and beef could appear in many dishes; the best known was kielbasa, which simply means sausage. Most families made their own, using recipes passed down from father to son. Flavors varied by region and family, but garlic, pepper, sage, and (in southeastern Poland) marjoram were the most common seasonings. Geese, chickens, and ducks were kept by most rural families and provided meat, feathers (for the winter comforters called pierzina), and eggs.

Nearly every Polish garden had potatoes, peas, asparagus, cucumbers (for pickles), dill, and cabbage. Farm families also planted fruit trees—apples at a minimum, but also plums and pears. Mushrooms were an absolute necessity, and mushroom hunting was a ritual brought from the old country. Favorite mushrooming locations were closely guarded secrets. Another crucial ingredient was poppy seed, which was purchased at Polish grocery stores.

The high point in the culinary year was and continues to be the Christmas Eve dinner or *wigilia*. This intensive ritual begins with the appearance of the first evening star. The table is carefully set with a piece of straw beneath the tablecloth to symbolize Christ's birth in the stable, and an extra place is set for any uninvited guest. Dinner begins with *opłatek*, a square unleavened wafer (or unconsecrated communion wafer). Each family member shares a piece of his or her wafer with family members in turn (usually going from the oldest to the youngest), forgiving all conflicts of the past year and wishing each other a Merry Christmas and a prosperous new year. When Poles began to immigrate,

that were widely used. Because they had little mainstream media presence, many Polish Americans, especially young people, internalized these stereotypes. If students did not keep quiet, they faced harassment and abuse from classmates and sometimes even teachers. Within the Polish White Eagle Association, this stigmatization led to oc-

TREASURED *Polish* RECIPES

FOR AMERICANS

Cover of *Treasured Polish Recipes for Americans,* published by Polanie Club in 1948

the *opłatek* ritual was shared by mail by including the wafers in cards and letters sent to distant family or to relatives in the military service, symbolically recreating the unity of family. Next, the family would sit down to an odd number of dishes, all meatless. Clear barszcz with mushroom dumplings, pickled herring with chopped onions, and some form of pierogi were usually on the menu, though the choices varied from family to family. Following dinner, the family sang Christmas carols and then, well fortified against the winter night, proceeded to midnight Mass. After church, families returned home to enjoy a snack (this time with meat) before retiring.

After Polish sausage, pierogi became the best-known Polish dish, though few are aware of the immense variety of pierogi. Pierogi arrived with the earliest Polish immigrants and stayed. Not so with another famous Polish dish, bigos, or hunter's stew, a savory mix of meat and cabbage. This dish, originally the province of the nobility, probably did not make an appearance in Minnesota until after World War II with the advent of a new wave of immigration.

No meal was complete without something to wash it down. Polish immigrants were beer drinkers and made beer at home as well as in local saloons and bars. Many also made wine and whiskey. Rye whiskey seems to have been preferred, perhaps due to its similarity to the rye vodka many had known in Poland. A common winter concoction was *krupnik* made with honey, spices, and a generous dose of pure alcohol (*spiritus*). This was considered both a form of drink and medicine for sufferers of the common cold.

casional pressure to remove the word "Polish" from the group's name as early as the late 1960s.[78]

At the same time, there was an ethnic revival in the 1970s and a renewed interest in personal ethnicity, community history, and genealogy. Polish folk arts, especially folk dancing, saw a resurgence in popularity. Poles in Minnesota led a significant effort to microfilm Polish American newspapers, coordinated by the Immigration History Research Center at the University of Minnesota. Czesław Róg founded a new community newsletter, *The Pol-Am,* in 1979. In Ivanhoe, a college professor joined local business leaders to launch Polska Kielbasa Days as the town's summer festivity. In Winona, Fr. Paul Breza started a Polish heritage society in 1976 that later grew to become the Polish Museum of Winona. There was also a short-lived effort to create a Polish-language Saturday school, which existed from 1977 to 1980.[79] Finally, the first history of Poles in Minnesota was written by Frank Renkiewicz of St. Theresa's College in Winona as part of the Minnesota Ethnic History Project.

Yet the most important event of this period was the election of a Polish cardinal as Pope John Paul II, which provided a key psychological boost to Polish Americans in Minnesota and elsewhere. Many felt it would signal the end of anti-Polish abuse from the media among others. Msgr. Stanisław Grabowski of Redwood Falls said, "Now we can look forward to GOOD Polish humor." A Polish activist in Minneapolis, Edmund Lukaszewski, told a local paper, "I am so sick of those screwy Polack jokes that I said a Hail Mary (prayer) that for once this stupid Polack thing can come to rest because now there is an internationally respected Polish official.... We finally made it." John Paul II's election sparked the rise of the Solidarity movement in Poland and the beginning of the end of Communism in Europe. Sympathizers from all walks

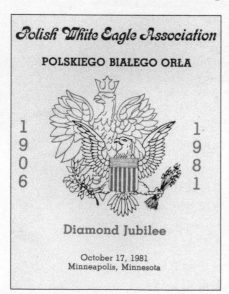

Polish White Eagle Association

POLSKIEGO BIAŁEGO ORLA

1906

1981

Diamond Jubilee

October 17, 1981
Minneapolis, Minnesota

Souvenir book of the Polish White Eagle Association's 75th anniversary. This Minnesota fraternal society had about 20 chapters across the state.

Procession at St. Adalbert Catholic Church, St. Paul, celebrating the millennium of Poland's conversion to Christianity, 1966

of life joined Poles in Minnesota in providing moral and material support to victims of the Communist crackdown against the movement. One result was an effort to revive the Polish Centralia, which resulted in the creation of the Polish American Cultural Institute Minnesota (PACIM) in the mid-1980s.[80] The momentous changes in Europe in the late 1980s and early 1990s also resulted in a wave of new Polish arrivals in the North Star State.

In 1980, the census estimated more than 200,000 Minnesotans were of Polish ancestry, of whom 63,000 named

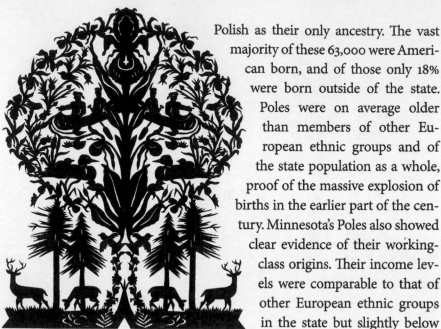

Emeline Dziabas Cook is an artist in wycinanki (Polish paper cutting). She follows the tradition of cutting the paper in a continuous pattern for *Leluja* (Tree-of-Life), which uses themes from Minnesota.

Polish as their only ancestry. The vast majority of these 63,000 were American born, and of those only 18% were born outside of the state. Poles were on average older than members of other European ethnic groups and of the state population as a whole, proof of the massive explosion of births in the earlier part of the century. Minnesota's Poles also showed clear evidence of their working-class origins. Their income levels were comparable to that of other European ethnic groups in the state but slightly below the state average. The legacy of being a disadvantaged ethnic group and the collective family choices of the older generation that had emphasized reliable blue-collar jobs over education was most evident in Poles' lower-than-average rate of high school graduation, a situation not unlike that of Latino communities in the 1990s. The great majority of Minnesota Poles traced their origins to the pre-World War I migration, though there was an active group of post-World War II immigrants and a smattering of families who had managed to leave Communist-dominated Poland after the death of Soviet tyrant Stalin, the most famous of whom was Stanisław Skrowaczewski, who became the conductor of the Minnesota Orchestra.

By the mid-1980s, however, this picture began to change once again. As the situation in Poland evolved, many of those active in the Solidarity movement were forced into exile. Most were well educated, and a significant proportion had advanced degrees. Although Minnesota was not a prime destination of this migration, from 500 to perhaps 1,000 new Polish immigrants came to the state during the

European Single Ancestry Groups in the U.S. Census, 1980, Minnesota[81]						
	English	French	German	Irish	Italian	Polish
Number	109,486	38,943	707,161	96,187	20,853	63,518
Pct. Foreign Born	5.1%	3.5%	1.6%	1.9%	8.6%	4.1%
Pct. Born in MN	94.8%	70.9%	78.6%	65.0%	60.1%	78.3%
Median Age (M)	38.1	38.9	34.9	39.0	40.3	41.8
Median Age (F)	40.5	40.6	36.0	42.0	41.4	43.8
High School Grads (M)	76.4%	63.0%	63.6%	76.0%	72.8%	60.8%
High School Grads (F)	76.8%	65.3%	66.0%	77.2%	71.6%	58.9%
Median Family Income	$21,815	$20,115	$20,280	$21,884	$23,627	$21,097
Mean Family Income	$26,706	$22,465	$22,649	$25,780	$26,273	$23,501
Employed in Agriculture*	4.3%	3.1%	10.2%	3.2%	0.9%	5.8%
Employed in Manufact.*	21.2%	21.5%	21.5%	18.3%	18.6%	24.6%
*Of persons employed age 16 and over						

mid- to late 1980s, though not all stayed. The University of Minnesota attracted some, while others found jobs in Minnesota companies, often as engineers and researchers. After the fall of Communism in Poland in 1989, even more Poles immigrated to Minnesota, some directly, others via larger receiving cities such as Chicago or New York. Poles arriving in the 1990s tended to be economic immigrants, though some were students or participants in family-reunion programs.

The new blood brought further changes to Minnesota Polonia. Although the newcomers did not settle in any geographically defined area, they made use of the Polish hub at Holy Cross in Minneapolis, which revived the use of Polish in the parish and strengthened the Polish ministry there. To serve this group, as well as older Polish-speaking parishioners, priests from the Poznań-based Society of Christ were introduced to the parish as associate pastors in 1981. In 1991, new Polish immigrants at Holy Cross created the Adam Mickiewicz Saturday School, with instruction that included language, culture, history, and catechism.[82]

The integration of these newcomers into a well-established parish did not occur without difficulty. The

Something of Their Very Own to Say

From almost the beginning of Polish settlement in Minnesota, creative writing has been a special contribution of the state's Polonia. In the 1880s, Hieronym Derdowski founded the weekly *Wiarus*. By the time of his death in 1902, he was recognized as the great poet of the Kaszub dialect (a Slavic language closely related to Polish and spoken by the inhabitants of Poland's Baltic Coast region). Derdowski published poetry, devotional works, polemics, and a Polish-Kaszub dictionary. *Wiarus* also provided a forum for the creative impulses of some of Derdowski's fellow immigrants. In the years before World War I, the newspaper published a huge number of poems, essays, polemics, and correspondence from readers across Minnesota and the Midwest.

The second and third generation also produced writers of note, despite having to make the difficult transition from Polish to English. Both Wiktoria Janda and Monika Krawczyk were reared in America and were founding members of the Polanie Club. Janda published three collections of poetry in the 1940s and 1950s and was nominated for a Pulitzer Prize for *Singing Furrows*. Krawczyk wrote short stories and was the author of *If the Branch Blossoms* (1950). Janda served as president of the League of Minnesota Poets and belonged to the National League of American Pen Women. They were among the first writers to explore the intersection of gender and ethnicity.

In the decades since, other Polish American writers—both native Minnesotans and transplants—have taken up where Janda and Krawczyk left off. Two anthologies of Polish American writing published in Minnesota had heavy Minnesota representation. Poets such as John Minczeski, Mark Nowak, and John Calvin Rezmerski continue this tradition. Winona children's author Anne Pellowski, an internationally recognized storyteller, has written and edited more than 15 books.

Ironically, despite being pioneers in Minnesota ethnic literature, writers like Janda and Krawczyk have been ignored by the state's literary set and do not appear on lists of the state's notable women. As one scholar recently wrote, however, "Janda reminded America of its multicultural nature and of its social and moral obligation to its many voices when she wrote these words:

> To you who claim your sires among
> The bards of English lore,
> And stand aloof because they walked
> Upon an ocean shore
> . . . .
> To you, I now have something of
> My very own to say."

immigrants had come from a Poland very different from the homeland of the earlier generation, and there were sharp contrasts in class and educational level. Just as in the case of the World War II generation, the newcomers viewed the existing parishioners as too Americanized and unwelcoming, while the latter saw the former as arrogant and standoffish. Beginning in the late 1980s, there were a series of community conflicts between the older Polish American parishioners and the new arrivals. This situation was exacerbated in several instances by the archdiocese, which seemed no more welcoming to Poles than in Archbishop Ireland's day. The most serious disruption occurred in 1996–97 when the archdiocese suggested ending the Society of Christ's relationship with the parish and replacing the younger assistant pastor with a retired priest, which was tantamount to closing the Polish ministry. This move resulted in a parish revolt and a protest demonstration by 250 parishioners outside the chancery offices in St. Paul. The upshot was that the Polish ministry remained, though tensions within the parish took longer to calm.[83]

If the dispute at Holy Cross was an unhappy reminder of past conflicts, the 1990s also provided examples of how the Polish community could adapt and change. Community groups made more serious efforts to include both new and old immigrants. Common goals provided a basis for cooperation. One example was the effort to lobby

Nativity play put on by students at the Adam Mickiewicz Polish Saturday School, Minneapolis, 2003

Minnesota's U.S. Senators to support Poland's entry into NATO. Local activists undertook a successful petition drive, organized letter-writing campaigns, and helped secure resolutions of support from both the Minnesota House and Senate. Fourth-generation Polish Americans worked closely with new immigrants and joined forces with local Czech and Hungarian organizations as well. While newer immigrants could be counted on for support, older communities showed that they had not forgotten the land of their ancestors. Poles in Silver Lake, for example, signed the NATO petition en masse more than a century after their ancestors had come from Poland. The lobbying paid off in helping to secure the vote of one of Minnesota's two senators.[84]

A free Poland in an age of mass communication and easy air travel provided immigrants much greater access to their homeland than in previous generations. This allowed Poles in Minnesota to develop new relationships with Poland, often using the institutional contacts and bases they had developed in Minnesota. For example, the University of Minnesota's Hubert H. Humphrey Institute of Public Affairs developed a joint master's degree program with the University of Warmia and Mazury in Olsztyn, an effort that was spearheaded by an émigré professor at the institute. Minnesota-based Land O' Lakes Corporation opened operations in Poland in response to grass-roots advocacy among its farmer-members of Polish descent in Minnesota and Wisconsin.

Although anti-Polish insults did not go away, as shown by a 1996 article in the fashionable *Minnesota Monthly*, and Poles and other white ethnics are routinely omitted from the pantheon of "diversity," the situation of the state's Polish Americans improved in the 1980s and 1990s.[85] Nowhere was this better demonstrated than in the U.S. Census ancestry self-identification. In 1980, some 200,000 Minnesotans had listed Polish ancestry. In 2000, without major in-migration, this number jumped to almost 260,000.

Since 1905, observers both inside and outside the Polish community in the United States have predicted its imminent demise. Yet Polish Americans continue to confound the experts. The Polish community of Minnesota, with its relatively small size compared to major centers such as Chicago or Detroit, remains in existence. But it is no longer a community defined by geography. The proportion of active community members to those who identify as Polish Americans on the census is small. Old fraternal societies are a shadow of their former selves. The Polish White Eagle Association dropped its Polish name in the 1990s, but its old-generation leaders lost faith in the idea that a Polish fraternal organization had any future whatsoever, and in

Corpus Christi procession at Holy Cross Catholic Church, June 2003

2001 it merged with a non-Polish rival.[86] Newer immigrants, while highly motivated and intensely ethnic, often retain a strong aversion to joining associations, perhaps due to formative years lived in a totalitarian socialist state. Their primary social groups are small clusters of friends who often work well in pursuit of common goals but have little formal structure.

Newer societies, such as PACIM and the Polish Genealogical Society of Minnesota, have emerged to help create and sustain a sense of history and community. Despite the modest size of some of the organizations, when pressed by crisis or presented with opportunities to help Poland—a land that many have never seen—the response is often overwhelming. A drive to aid Polish orphanages, spread almost entirely by word of mouth, resulted in tons of clothing, supplies, and money being sent to Poland. As the new century begins, Poles in Minnesota represent a kind of virtual community, held together by a core of dedicated activists and groups who are able on occasion to mobilize significant support for common goals. Although much in the life of Polish Americans in Minnesota has changed, the community's present finds continuing echoes in its past. In 1908, correspondents from St. Paul greeted their brethren in Chicago and Winona with a paraphrase from the Polish national anthem. The words recalled that their identity and their culture could endure even without an independent state. As long as Poles survived, Poland would not die: "Poland is not yet lost in the far west," they wrote, "at least not in our city of St. Paul." As philosopher Jaroslav Pelikan noted, "Tradition is the living faith of the dead."[87] Although their descendants are firmly American, the continuing survival and persistence of Polish American culture gives proof that what was bequeathed to them by their ancestors yet lives.

Personal Account:
Reminiscences from Lincoln County

by Katherine Górecki-Ross

Katherine Górecki-Ross was the daughter of two of the first Polish settlers in Lincoln County in southwestern Minnesota. Her parents, Jakub and Róża Górecki, were both from the Poznan region of western Poland. They were probably married in the Chicago area in the late 1870s after immigrating to the United States. In 1883, Jakub and Róża joined a colony created by the Polish National Alliance, one of the leading Polish organizations in the U.S. By the time Katherine was born in 1893, Jakub and Róża were among the leaders of the Lincoln County Polish community. They passed on to their daughter a wealth of information about the early days of Polish settlement. Katherine, who later married Marcel Ross (Roszkowski), had an extraordinary ability to recall both the stories she learned from her parents and her own memories of growing up Polish American in rural Minnesota.

So then they started this little parish and built a little house for the priest. They got a priest Father Kosiolek; he was the first pastor. For the first mass he said, my mother furnished the linens. She had a linen tablecloth from the old country that was homespun. They used that and she took a Blessed Virgin picture and the first mass was said on that, after they had organized. She served the first loaf of bread. The men brought in straw and they made a bed for this priest and he slept on the floor. My mother furnished sheets for him. That was for Father Koziolek. He didn't stay too long. It was from March to July 1883. He was an order priest—a Franciscan, Chicago.

They [her father and mother] donated the cemetery in Wilno, the railroad. They had a hard time in Wilno. They had a lot of fights and everything. Some of them had sod houses. Not us, we had a house. We saved money. We were king of the rich people, from the rich-poor. In the wintertime, they couldn't even bury them—they couldn't even dig the graves in the cemetery—they had to leave them until spring. They had bad winters at that time.

The first church they didn't have much difficulty, but when they built

Jakub and Róża Górecki and three generations of their family, Limestone Township, Lincoln County, 1910. Jakub and Róża, at lower right, were among the founders of the Polish community in the county and the parents of Katherine Ross.

the brick building they had a priest there, and I don't know what happened; they ended up short of money. He spent the money, and they had lots of fights over it.

The priest took off. We used to go to school and used to jump on top of that church foundation. Then after a while they got this Jupe; he was the man who built the new foundation. When they moved the old church from one place so they wanted to make room for the new church. They used horses. My father wasn't secretary any more, and when they built the new church and they got into such a *frickus* and they came and took him on their backs because he was crippled, and he had to come and help them. They carried him to the meetings. . . .

Katherine attended the Polish school; classes were in Polish in the morning and in English in the afternoon. Father Czeminski brought in Franciscan sisters to teach.

They were from Rochester. Their house was really the first priest's house. When they built the new priest's house, they moved the old one way behind, down further, and the sisters occupied it. The old church, that was the school that we had. . . .

We didn't like to go to the parish school because it was strict. But my mother and father used to tell us that since father was church secretary he thought he had to go to the parish every Sunday even when we had storms, and we used to have such storms. Even though he had to go by oxen my Pa always thought he had to go. Once shortly after the parish was founded, when the second priest was there, Fr. Jerzewski [Jeżdżew-ski], he [my father] took a stoneboat and he took the oxen. Those oxen went—we were two miles straight east of Wilno—and they went and my pa lost his cap and the oxen wouldn't stop until he got right to Wilno, and they said that the priest and others were out there, and they just laughed. Pa came without his cap because the oxen wouldn't stop until he got to Wilno. And all the while it was snowing terribly.

Ma always laughed, she always had to laugh whenever she thought about it. Because he really didn't have to go, because it stormed so hard, but those oxen found a way. They went straight over the snow. Oh, yeah, those were hard times, oh my goodness, those were hard times. But they enjoyed it. They had their doings, you know. And the father, Jerzewski, he was a really good priest. He build the altar himself as well as the pulpit. He was the priest who was later murdered at Holy Cross parish, the Polish parish in the Cities. I was there, I worked as a housekeeper. I saw her—the woman who murdered him. She was a górala, she came from the Gorale, from the mountains [in southern Poland]. Oh yes, that was too bad, you know. He baptized me when he was in Wilno.

They had lots of parties . . . house parties when they would have christenings. Then they'd play fresz box, they called it a fresz box. They had a cap, and they would select some man from the bunch, and then they'd put the head in that cap and pull it over his eyes and some man would go and give him a fresz box, that is punch him. He would have to guess who did it. Until he did, they would hit him. Once my dad was the one in there, and this Fr. Jerzewski kept hitting him, and he couldn't guess and he couldn't guess and he got so many of those fresz boxes my mother said they had to laugh because he didn't think that it was the priest. That was the fun they had . . . at these parties.

The church records indicated that the church ran a boardinghouse.

There were so many people who lived so far away, and in the winter-time, there were blizzards. My mother also had a lot of kids in her house. After they retired, they lived across from the church, and she had, oh I don't know how many, she had her own, my brother's children, John had his kids there, and from Taunton, too, Lozinskis, two or three of them went to school there. She had quite a bunch. She took care of the kids who lived in the country and went to school in town.

The boardinghouse, the sisters took care of that. But that was in later years.

The customs and the foods carried over from the Old Country.

We never ate meat on Wigilia. That was advent. We didn't eat meat until Christmas. Then, of course, on Christmas we would have lots of duck. We baked, like cookies. [We would eat] some fish. But we didn't always have fish. . . . And kasha. We always had Opłatek. That was at midnight. When we would come home from church, then we broke them. After midnight Mass. Mother would start it, and we each would take a little. . . . I loved to do it. It is a good custom.

[On Christmas Day,] we would go to church, and then eat most of the day. We would have czarnina [duck soup] then. And a lot of baked stuff. We always had coffee cake. [We would have] babka and sometimes my mother would fill it with cottage cheese. It was so good. Very thick on top. And pies we would have, too, mostly apple pies because it was the cheapest. And we would have different biscuits. . . .

When my mother made cookies or bread, she'd bake about fifteen loaves of bread. . . . We had pans, they were big ones, put a lot of loaves of bread in there.

[We baked] white. . . . We baked dark bread, too. We had rye, you know we raised rye and then ground it up. We liked rye bread, especially, [when] mother put raisins in it sometimes. And we like rye bread. It even tasted good if it was old.

Most of the social life in the early years revolved around the home. Often the parties involved card games.

Oh, cards! They played cards—sixty-six, dog (pies), Oklahoma, games like that. My dad lost his beard one time playing cards. He [father] went to Bednareks; that was just before Lent. I suppose they were drinking a little bit, you know, having a good time. Maybe, they had some schnapps, too. So Bednarek says, let's play for the beards. And by golly my dad lost his beard. And he came home, and he didn't have any beard. My mother was so mad. She wasn't along that time. He looked so funny. . . .

They didn't have all those social doings in church then. When we went to church, we went with horses and had to put them somewhere. So they built barns in Wilno for the church. They had . . . big long barns where they each one built their own section and paid for it themselves. When they came to Wilno, then they unhitched the horses and put them in the barn.

Source: Interview of Katherine Górecki-Ross by Thaddeus C. Radzilowski at her home in Taunton, Minn., Aug. 24, 1972, Southwest Minnesota Regional Research Center, Southwest Minnesota State University, Marshall, Minn.

For Further Reading

Bukowczyk, John J. *And My Children Did Not Know Me: A History of the Polish Americans.* Bloomington: Indiana University Press, 1987.

Bukowczyk, John J., ed. *Polish Americans and Their History: Community, Culture, and Politics.* Pittsburgh: Pittsburgh University Press, 1996.

Gladsky, Thomas S., and Rita Holmes Gladsky, eds. *Something of My Very Own to Say: American Women Writers of Polish Descent.* New York: East European Monographs/Columbia University Press, 1997.

Holmquist, June D., ed. *They Chose Minnesota: A Survey of the State's Ethnic Groups.* St. Paul: Minnesota Historical Society Press, 1981.

Kruszka, Waclaw. *A History of the Poles in America to 1908,* 4 vols., James S. Pula, ed., Krystyna Jankowski, trans. Washington, D.C.: Catholic University of America Press, 1993–2002.

Kula, Witold, Nina Assorodobraj-Kula, Marcin Kula, and Josephine Wtulich, eds. *Writing Home: Immigrants in Brazil and the United States, 1890–1891,* Josephine Wtulich, trans. Boulder, Colo.: East European Monographs, 1986.

Pula, James S. *Polish Americans: An Ethnic Community.* New York: Twayne, 1995.

Radzilowski, John. *The Eagle and the Cross: A History of the Polish Roman Catholic Union of America.* New York: East European Monographs/Columbia University Press, 2003.

Notes

1. Parulski's story is based on the author's interviews with his daughter, Rose Parulski, of Ivanhoe, Minn., as well as tax and census records and parish histories. See John Radziłowski, "Hidden Cosmos: The Life World of Polish Immigrants in Two Minnesota Communities,1875–1925," Ph.D. diss., Arizona State University,1999.

2. U.S. *Census,* 2000, ancestry figures.

3. Radzilowski, "Hidden Cosmos," 88–107; James S. Pula, *Polish Americans: An Ethnic Community* (New York, 1995), 14–19.

4. Stanisław Bilanski settled in what is now St. Paul in 1842. He died under mysterious circumstances in 1859, and his Anglo wife was convicted of murder and became the only woman ever executed in Minnesota. See J. Fletcher Williams, *A History of the City of St. Paul to 1875* (1876; St. Paul,1983),121–22,199; Matthew Cecil, "Justice in Heaven: The Trial of Ann Bilansky [sic]," *Minnesota History* 55 (Winter 1997–98): 350–63.

5. F[ranciszek J.] Niklewicz, *Polacy w Stanach Zjednoczonych* [Poles in the United States] (Green Bay,1937),17–20,26, 34; Frank Renkiewicz, research notes on the history of Poles in Minnesota, uncatalogued copy, Central Archives of Polonia, Orchard Lake Schools, Orchard Lake, Mich.; Parish History Questionnaires, 1949, chancery archives, Archdiocese of St. Paul and Minneapolis; John Radzilowski, *Out on the Wind: Poles and Danes in Lincoln County, Minnesota, 1880–1905* (Marshall, 1992), 72, 74; Pine County, Sturgeon Lake, Manuscript census,1900; *Św. Jozefa, Lexington, Minnesota, 1902–2002* ([Montgomery], 2002). On Polish Lutherans, see *Fiftieth Anniversary Trinity Evangelical Lutheran Church,1887–1957,* p. 8, Churches file, Minnesota Ethnic History Project (hereafter MEHP), MHS.

6. According to Paul Libera, the first Poles arrived in 1855; Libera, "History of the Polish People at Winona, Minnesota," typescript of address to the Winona County Historical Society, Oct. 26, 1955, p. 3–4, copy in MHS, and "Polish Settlers in Winona, Minnesota," *Polish American Studies* 15 (Jan.–June 1958): 18–29; *Diamond Jubilee Memoirs, 1873–1948: St. Stanislaus Kostka Parish, Winona, Minnesota* (Winona, 1948), 23; T. Kukliński, Stevens Point, Wis., to Antoni Kochanek, Milwaukee, Jan. 30,1864, typescript in file "Poles: Winona," MEHP; Władysław Szulist, "Z Przeszłości Kaszubskiej Emigracji w Winonie," *Przegląd Polonijny* 15 (1989): 97–108; Shirley Mask Connolly, "Your Canadian Kashub Cousins and Their Trek from Wilno to Winona," *Polish Genealogical Society of Minnesota Newsletter* (hereafter *PGSMN*), Summer 1995, 5–9.

7. *Delano: Founded 1868, Incorporated 1876* (Delano, [ca. 1976]); *Church of St. Mary, Czestochowa, 1884–1984* (Delano, 1984), 9; *Nowiny Minnesockie,* July 20,1923, Sept. 1,1922, July 13,1923; Wacław Kruszka, *Historia Polska w Ameryce* (Milwaukee, 1907), 11:9–14; "Krótki rys historyczno-statystyczny osady polskiej Silver Lake" *Przegląd Emigracyjny* (Lwów), April 15, 1894, 76–77; entry for St. Adalbert's Parish, Silver Lake, *Polish American Encyclopedia* (Buffalo, 1954), 49–50; *Church of the Holy Family* (Silver Lake, 1995), 3–4.

8. John Radziłowski, "A New Poland in the Old Northwest: Polish Farming Communities on the Northern Great Plains," *Polish American Studies* 59 (Autumn 2002): 79–96; Robert J. Voight, *Opoliana, 1887–1987: A History of the Community of Opole, Minnesota* (Opole, 1987), 12 (quote); *The Kashubian Polish Community of Southeastern Minnesota* (Chicago, 2001); Leo M. Ochrymowycz, "The Polish People of Southeastern Minnesota: Ethnic Heritage," in *Lectures on Perspectives on Regionalism*, Ahmed El-Afandi, ed. (Winona, [mid-1970s]); *History of St. Casimir's Catholic Church Winona, Minn.* (undated copy in author's files). On New Brighton, see Wacław Kruszka, *A History of Poles in America to 1908*, Part 4: *The Central and Western States*, James S. Pula, ed., Krystyna Jankowski, trans. (Washington, D.C., 2001), 121; Rosina Boryczka and Janet Boryczka Johnson, *St. John the Baptist Catholic Church: A Pictorial History* (New Brighton, 1983). On Holloway, see *Wiarus*, April 16, 1891, p. 4–5, March 26, 1896, p. 8; *St. Joseph's Catholic Church, Holloway, Minnesota, 1887–1987* (Appleton, 1987); *Appleton Press*, April 29, 1992, p.1, 3.

9. Jeanette Bias, "Silesian Polish Settlements in South Central Minnesota," *PGSMN*, Autumn 2000, p. 1, 8–11; *St. Casimir's Church, Wells, Minnesota, Centennial, June 1985* (Wells, 1985); *Wells Centennial, 1869–1969* (Wells, 1969), 30–33; Kruszka, *Historia Polska w Ameryce*, 4: 116–18; *Church of St. Mary, Czestochowa,* 9–11; *Golden Jubilee, 1904–1954, Church of St. Joseph, Delano, Minnesota* (Delano, 1954). On the architect, see Geoffrey M. Gyrisco, "Victor Cordella and the Architecture of Polish and East Slavic Identity in America," *Polish American Studies* 54 (Spring 1997): 33–52.

10. Radziłowski, "A New Poland in the Old Northwest," and *The Eagle and the Cross: A History of the Polish Roman Catholic Union of America, 1873–2000* (New York, 2003), esp. 61–66; *Minneapolis Tribune*, Nov. 27, 1877; *Nowiny Minnesockie*, Aug. 29, 1924; *Sauk Rapids Sentinel*, Dec. 25, 1877. On *Przyjaciel Ludu*, see Kruszka, *Historia Polska w Ameryce*, 1:268–70.

11. Radziłowski, "Hidden Cosmos," 118–88, and *Out on the Wind*. Extant copies of *Gazeta Chicagoska* are found in Biblioteka Kórnik, Kórnik, Poland.

12. Radziłowski, "Hidden Cosmos," 107–88.

13. *Wiarus*, Feb. 11, 1891, p. 5, Mar. 19, 1896, p. 8, Oct. 25, 1900, p. 4; *Gazeta Polska Narodowa* (Chicago), Mar. 21, 1895, p. 4, Mar. 21, 1895, p. 4, Apr. 1, 1895, p. 3, May 23, 1895, p. 1; *Red Lake Rezerwacya i Red River Dolina w Minnesocie* (1896), promotional pamphlet, 132.D.19.10, folder 1, Great Northern Railroad Co., Land Department Records, MHS; *Holy Rosary Church, Lancaster, Minnesota, 1900–1975* (Lancaster, 1975); entries for St. Aloysius Parish, Leo, and Assumption Parish, Florian, *Polish American Encyclopedia*, 110, 305–6; *Silver Jubilee 1950–1975, Assumption Catholic Church of Florian* (Florian, 1975). For typical ads, see *Wiarus*, June 14, Aug. 23, 1888, May 31, Aug. 15, 1889—all p. 5.

14. *Wiarus*, Dec. 27, 1889, p. 1.

15. *Gazeta Polska Narodowa*, May 23, 1895, p. 1.

16. Charles B. Lamborn to C. B. Richard & Co., Mar. 24, 1893, 137.K.14.1b, box 1, vol. 4, p. 253–54, William Phipps, to Thomas Cooper, Feb. 9, 1897, 137.K.15.4F, box 12, vol. 57, p. 649, J. F. Hughes, to G. H. Plummer, Jan. 29, 1929, and May 6, 1929, 136.B.12.2(F), box 7, vols. 41 and 42—all

Northern Pacific Railroad Co., Land Department Records, MHS.

17. Radziłowski, "A New Poland in the Old Northwest," 79–80, 92–94; *Wiarus*, June 7, 1888; *Gazeta Polska Narodowa*, Mar. 15, 1888, p. 2.

18. Edward A. Chmielewski, "A History of Holy Cross Parish, Minneapolis, Minnesota, 1886–1914: A Polish-American Community," Master's thesis, St. Paul Seminary, 1960, p. 4; Radziłowski, "Hidden Cosmos," 195, 258.

19. Paul T. Kulas, "Polish Catholic Churches in Minnesota. Part 1: Polish Catholic Churches in the Archdiocese of St. Paul and Minneapolis," *PGSMN*, Spring 1994, p. 5–8; *Polish American Encyclopedia*, 58; *Centennial Celebration, 1881–1981: Church of St. Adalbert* (St. Paul, 1981), 21; Kruszka, *History of Poles in America*, 4:114–15.

20. Radziłowski, "Hidden Cosmos," 196–98 and maps 4 and 5.

21. *St. Casimir Catholic Church, 1892–1982* (St. Paul, 1982); *Wiarus*, Dec. 8, 1892, p. 8; Kruszka, *History of Poles in America*, 4:115–16; "St. Casimir's Church and Its 100-Year Journey of Faith," *Ramsey County History* 27 (Fall 1992): 22–23; Radziłowski, "Hidden Cosmos," 259–60; *Nowiny Minnesockie*, Apr. 7, 1922.

22. Radzilowski, "Hidden Cosmos," 193–98; Calvin F. Schmid, *Social Saga of Two Cities: An Ecological and Statistical Study of Social Trends in Minneapolis and St. Paul* (Minneapolis, 1937), chart 77.

23. Chmielewski, "Holy Cross Parish," 4, 7; WPA Writer's Program, *The Bohemian Flats* (St. Paul, 1986).

24. Kruszka, *History of Poles in America*, 4:116; *Diamond Jubilee, Church of the Holy Cross, Minneapolis, Minnesota, 1886–1961* (Minneapolis, 1961); *Nowiny Minnesockie*, June 23, 1922.

25. Genny Zak Kieley, *Heart and Hard Work: Memories of "Nordeast" Minneapolis* (Minneapolis, 1997), 127. Biennas' Polish was laced with Slovak, as shown by sayings like "Ya stanzas Bogum" (Go with God); standard Polish would be "Z Bogiem." A member of the Biennas family was an officer in the local branch of the PNA; see Polish National Alliance Council 1435, Minute Book, 1920–35, p. 12, IHRC.

26. *Church of St. Philip, Minneapolis, Minnesota: 75th Anniversary, 1906–1981* (Minneapolis, 1981), 2; *Church of St. Hedwig, Minneapolis, Minnesota, 1914–1964* (Minneapolis, 1964), 20, 22; *Polish American Encyclopedia*, 106–8.

27. Kruszka, *History of Poles in America*, 4:133–35; "Churches" file and *Catholic Directory of Duluth, 1892*, MEHP. The English name is usually St. Mary, Star of the Sea. Ed Jankowski, *St. Casimir's Roman Catholic Church (Queen of Peace Chapel), Cloquet, Minnesota, 1910–1994* (Cloquet, 1994); Greg Kishel, "Z Lesnictwa Raigrodzkiego: A Chain Migration from Poland's North Country to Minnesota's Mesabi Iron Range," Summer 2001, p. 8–14, "Patterns of Polish Settlement in Minnesota, 1910: Buyck Township," Winter 1998–99, p. 10–17, "A Visit to Buyck," Summer 1999, p. 1, 20—all *PGSMN*.

28. *Reports of the U.S. Immigration Commission, 1907–1910*, 61st Cong., 2d sess., *Fecundity of Immigrant Women* (Washington, 1911), 28:786–92.

29. Radzilowski, *Out on The Wind*, 53, and "Hidden Cosmos," 152–54, 194, 200–201; Voight, *Opoliana*, 20.

30. *Reports of the U.S. Immigration Commission, 1907–1910, Immigrants in Industry: Recent Immigrants in Agriculture*, 22:181, 192; Radziłowski, "Hidden

Cosmos," 139–42; *Lake Benton News,* May 10, 1893, p. 4 (quote); Eleanor Simon, *The Story of a Polish Family* (Owatonna, 1995), 5.

31. Radziłowski, "Hidden Cosmos," 139, 150–53, 155–56; Nancy Dolum, ed. *Self Portrait of Marshall County* (Dallas, 1976), 790, 792–93.

32. Katherine Górecki-Ross, interview by Thaddeus Radzilowski, Aug. 24, 1972, transcript, Southwest Minnesota Regional Research Center, Marshall.

33. Thaddeus C. Radzilowski, "Reinventing the Center: Polish Immigrant Women in the New World," in *Something of My Very Own to Say: American Women Writers of Polish Descent,* Thomas S. Gladsky and Rita Holmes Gladsky, eds. (New York, 1997), 14.

34. Radziłowski, "Hidden Cosmos," 241–67.

35. *Wiarus,* Dec. 2, 1886, p. 4 (quote), Dec. 22, 1904, p. 1; M[anuel] C[onrad] Elmer, *The Juvenile Delinquent in Saint Paul, Minnesota: A Summary of Study* (St. Paul, 1926), 20–21; Northeast Neighborhood House Records, Box 4, Head Worker's Reports, Jan., Feb., Apr. 1916, MHS; Radziłowski, "Hidden Cosmos," 179–84. See also John Radziłowski, "Crime, Delinquency, Deviance, and Reform in Polish Chicago, 1890s–1940s," *Fiedorczyk Lecture in Polish American Studies* (New Britain, Conn., 2004).

36. Jankowski, *St. Casimir's Roman Catholic Church,* 4.

37. [Gene Retka,] *St. Stanislaus Parish, Sobieski, Minnesota: Centennial, 1884–1984* (Sobieski, 1984), 20, 21.

38. *Lake Benton News,* June 7, 1893, p. 4.

39. *Wiarus,* Feb. 2, 1893, p. 4; *Lake Benton News,* Feb. 1, 1893, p. 1.

40. *Wiarus,* July 1, 1886, p. 4.

41. Ibid., July 8, 1886, p. 4–5.

42. Ibid., Dec. 8, 1892, p. 4. See also *Zgoda* [Duluth], May 14, 1890, p. 4–5, Dec. 1890, p. 4.

43. *Wiarus,* May 15, 1891, p. 1.

44. Ibid., Feb. 18, 1897, p. 1; *St. Hyacinth's Roman Catholic Church, La Salle, Illinois* (La Salle, 1950), 39.

45. *Wiarus,* Mar. 25, 1897, p. 1; *Lake Benton News,* Mar. 17, 1897, p. 1; Radziłowski, "Hidden Cosmos," 167–71; Renkiewicz, "The Poles," 370–72.

46. *St. Josephat's Polish National Catholic Church, Forty-year Anniversary, 1907–1947* (Duluth, 1948); *St. Josephat's Polish National Catholic Church, Golden Anniversary, 1907–1957* (Duluth, 1957); Renkiewicz, "The Poles," 372. See also Fr. Francis Bolek Papers, Central Archives of Polonia. For the PNCC, see Pula, *Polish Americans,* 38–44. Independent churches were formed in Pierz (1919) and Foley (1913, but joined PNCC in 1917). A small PNCC chapel also existed in Split Rock Township, Carlton County; U.S., *Census of Religious Bodies: 1926* (Washington, 1930), 1:339.

47. Renkiewicz, "The Poles," 372; Bishop James Trobec, "Pastoral Letter for the Polish Parishes," April 1912, archives of the Diocese of St. Cloud.

48. Radziłowski, "Hidden Cosmos," 166.

49. Renkiewicz, "The Poles," 370. The Polish Franciscan sisters founded their own independent province in 1916 in Sylvania, Ohio, and thereafter most Polish sisters of Minnesota belonged to that motherhouse. See Thaddeus Radzilowski, "Immigrant Women and Their Daughters," Occasional Paper no. 16 in Polish and Polish American Studies, Central Connecticut State University, New Britain, 1990, p. 20–23.

50. Albert B. Clarfield, "The Americanization of the Foreign-born in Duluth: A Typical American Community," Master's thesis, University of Minnesota, 1920.

51. Edward A. Chmielewski, "Holy Cross Parish, Minneapolis, Minn., 1886–1906," *Polish American Studies* 13 (Jan.–June 1961): 6 (quote); *Katolik,* Mar. 1, 1894, p. 6. For constitutions, see *Wiarus,* May 15, 1891, p. 8 (Pułaski Legion, Winona), Feb. 4, 11, 1892 (St. Isidore Agricultural Circle, Sturgeon Lake), and July 17, 24, 31, 1890, p. 3 (Holy Cross Parish, Minneapolis); *Echo* (Buffalo), Oct. 17, 1895, p. 1 (Brotherhood of St. Casimir, Winona).

52. Radziłowski, *Eagle and the Cross,* 87–114.

53. The PNA Zgoda Society no. 22 had about 200 members in 1900. PNA Lodge [Society] no. 22 [Zgoda], Minneapolis, Minn., Minute Book, 1884–1909, and Polish White Eagle Association Records, IHRC.

54. *Zgoda,* July 14, 1898, p. 5, Nov. 13, 1889, p. 4; *Wiarus,* Dec. 3, 1896, p. 4; *Jutrzenka* (Pittsburgh), Sept. 1, 1894, p. 2.

55. *Wiarus,* June 28, 1888, p. 1; Radziłowski, *Out on the Wind,* 55–56.

56. Radzilowski, "Hidden Cosmos," 209.

57. *Zgoda,* April 19, 1893, p. 4, Jan. 24, 1894, p. 5, Jan. 30, 1896, p. 4–5, Mar. 26, 1896, p. 4, Jan. 20, 1898, p. 4, Feb. 2, 1899, p. 5, Feb. 9, 1899, p. 6; State of Minnesota, Secretary of State, Incorporation Records for Biblioteka Unia Lubelskiej, Dec. 5, 1894, book L2, p. 541, MHS; *St. Paul City Directory* (St. Paul, 1915), 118. The library collection eventually numbered about 500 books. The records of this library are in the collection of the IHRC. After World War II, the St. Paul Polish library was donated to the St. Paul Public Library, which accepted the books collected by the Polish community for decades and promptly discarded them; author's interview with Rose Polski-Anderson, St. Paul, Feb. 28, 1998, tape in author's possession.

58. Radziłowski, "Hidden Cosmos," 231–32, and *Out on the Wind,* 90; Stanislaus A. Blejwas, "American Polonia and the Wrzesnia School Strike," *Polish American Studies* 59 (Spring 2002): 9–59; *Wiarus,* Mar. 12, 1908, p. 5, Mar. 26, 1908, p. 1.

59. *Minneapolis Journal,* May 17, 1909, p. 14, May 6, 1907, p. 5.

60. Pula, *Polish Americans,* 53–66; Radziłowski, *Eagle and the Cross,* 147–60; Polish Citizens Committee, Center 20, Minneapolis, Minn., Correspondence, 1913–38, and Records, 1918–19, IHRC.

61. *Minneapolis Journal,* May 4, p. 11, May 9, p. 3, May 10, p. 11, May 13, p. 11, May 15, p. 5, May 16, p. 14—all 1915.

62. Ray Marshall, "The Polish Army in France in World War I (Haller's Army): Recruitment Database—Northern Minnesota," *PGSMN,* Autumn 2001, p. 1, 18–23. Renkiewicz's estimate of several hundred is obviously low; Renkiewicz, "The Poles," 373. The Polish Military Commission Recruiting Center 34 in Duluth was located at 22 5th Ave. W. For recruiting, see Polish Citizens Committee, Center 20, Records, 1918–19.

63. Northeast Neighborhood House Records, Box 4, Head Worker's Report, Apr. 1918, p. 1; *Minneapolis Journal,* Feb. 13, 1915, p. 1; Renkiewicz, "The Poles," 373; Radziłowski, *Eagle and the Cross,* 150–59.

64. *Ivanhoe Times,* May 2, 1919, p. 1, 4, Jan. 14, 1916, p. 1; *Nowiny Minnesockie,* Sept. 3, 1920; Polish Citizens Committee, Center 20, Records, 1918–19 (esp. p. 23, 88); "Daybook" (daily receipts) (Oct. 18, 1918), Polish National Department Records,

May 1918–May 1920, Polish Museum of America Archives, Chicago.

65. Adam Walaszek, "How Could It All Appear So Rosy? Re-emigrants from the United States in Poland," *Polish American Studies* 49 (Autumn 1992): 43–60; *Church of the Holy Cross, 1886–1986* (Minneapolis, 1986), 65–66.

66. *Nowiny Minnesockie,* Oct. 22, 1920; Polish National Department, Minneapolis, Minn., Minutes, 1931–1938 (Aug. 7, 1932, p. 58), IHRC.

67. PNA Lodge [Group] no. 1530 [Gwiazda Wolności], Minneapolis, Minn., Minutes, 1914–55, IHRC; *Pol-Am Newsletter,* Nov. 1997, p. 4–5.

68. PNA Lodge no. 1530, Minutes, 1914–24, p. 124–25; Gertrude Anderson, Polish folk customs in Duluth, April 30, 1936, Misc. folder, MEHP; "Zmiana na Centralę," Oct. 11, 1931, p. 42–43, Polish National Department, Minneapolis, and Minutes, 1931–1938 (Feb. 5, 1931, p. 182–83); *Minneapolis Journal,* Oct. 26, p. 26, Oct. 27, p. 1, Oct. 28, p. 11—all 1923. See also PNA Lodge no. 1530, Minutes, 1925–35 (Mar. 20, 1929).

69. Mary Jane Sokolowski-Gustafson Papers, uncatalogued, IHRC; Joseph Hart, "Notes of a Native Son," *City Pages,* Aug. 13, 1997, p. 13–18.

70. See, for example, *Duluth News Tribune,* Feb. 11, 22, Mar. 16, 1940; *Duluth Herald,* Jan. 20, Feb. 10, 16, 1940, Sept. 21, 1942.

71. John Radzilowski, "Polonia in World War II: Toward a Social History," *Polish American Studies* 58 (Spring 2001): 63–80. See also "Age of the Foreign Stock by Country of Origin: 1960," Bureau of the Census Supplementary Report PC (S1)-47, July 28, 1965.

72. Stanley Schmidt and Sally Smyrski, "Data on Polish-American Participation in World War II," *Polish American Studies* 58 (Autumn 2001): 81–96.

73. Parulski interviews; *Minneapolis Tribune,* Aug. 20, 1975, p. 1C, Dec. 25, 1977.

74. Anna Dorota [Jaroszyńska] Kirchmann, "'They Are Coming for Freedom, Not Dollars': Political Refugees and the Transformation of Ethnic Identity within the Polish-American Community after World War II," Ph.D. diss., University of Minnesota, 1997 (esp. p. 230); Msgr. Stanisław Grabowski, *Follow Me: The Memoirs of a Polish Priest,* John Radzilowski, ed. (Roseville, 1997); Walter Remiarz, "1994 Monte Cassino Celebration," July/Aug. 1994, p. 1–2, and Kazimierz Remiarz obituary, Dec. 1998, p. 2—both *Pol-Am Newsletter;* Michael Jaros, *Bukovinian and Galician Poles, 1895–1995* (Duluth, [1995]), 38–41.

75. www.dolina.org/history.htm; *Pol-Am Newsletter,* Oct. 1999, p. 4–5, Nov. 1999, p. 6.

76. *Centennial Celebration, 1881–1981: Church of St. Adalbert* (ad sec.).

77. Information from Fr. Gene Stenzel of Wells; Edmund Lukaszewski Papers, uncatalogued material, IHRC. Lukaszewski was a local activist and one of the last Polish-language teachers in the Minneapolis public schools.

78. John Bukowczyk, *And My Children Did Not Know Me: A History of the Polish Americans* (Bloomington, 1987); Thomas Napierkowski, "The Image of Polish Americans in American Literature," *Polish American Studies* 40 (Spring 1983): 5–44; Minutes, 1968 convention, Polish White Eagle Association Records, IHRC. On internalization of stereotypes, see the photographic collection from the Sobieski Polish days, early 1980s, MHS.

79. Frank Renkiewicz and Anne

Bjorkquist Ng, *Guide to Polish American Newspapers and Periodicals in Microform* (St. Paul, 1988); brochure, Polish Museum, Winona; *Pol-Am Newsletter*, Jan. 2002, p. 4–5; Wiesław Suszyński et al., eds. *Polska Szkoła im. Adama Mickiewicza w Minneapolis: 10 Lat Istnienia, 1991–2001* (Minneapolis, 2001), 6.

80. *Gwiazda Polarna*, Oct. 28, 1978, p. 3 (emphasis in original); *Minneapolis Star*, Oct. 17, 1978, p. 2A; www.pacim.org.

81. U.S., *Census, 1980, General Social and Economic Characteristics: Minnesota,* (Washington, 1980), 25:110–16; John Radzilowski, "Location of the Polish American Population, 1980–1990," *Polish American Historical Association Newsletter,* Summer 1996, p. 2–3. The state median income was $17,764 for households and $21,185 for families. For Poles, the comparable numbers were $17,457 for households and $21,097 for families.

82. Suszyński et al., eds. *Polska Szkoła im. Adama Mickiewicza,* 6–10.

83. A closed collection of papers relating to the situation at Holy Cross exists at the IHRC. There are additional documents in the author's possession. See also Mike Anderson, "Priest's Removal Rocks Holy Cross," *Northeaster,* Jan. 27, 1997, p. 1, 4–5; Beth Hawkins, "The Polish Inquisition," *City Pages,* Feb. 5, 1997, p. 7; *Pol-Am Newsletter,* Feb. 1997, p. 2; John Radzilowski, "Polish Americans Protest against Discrimination in St. Paul," *Polish American Journal,* Feb. 1997, p. 1.

84. Correspondence and copies of the petitions in author's possession. See also *Pol-Am Newsletter,* July–Aug. 1997, p. 4–5, 8.

85. *Minnesota Monthly,* Oct. 1995; *Pol-Am Newsletter,* March 1996, p. 2.

86. *Pol-Am Newsletter,* Nov. 2001, p. 1.

87. *Wiarus,* Dec. 10, 1908; Jaroslav Pelikan, *The Vindication of Tradition* (New Haven, 1984), 65.

Notes to Sidebars

Counting Poles, p. 3: Radzilowski, *Out on the Wind,* 117–22; "Age of the Foreign Stock by Country of Origin: 1960," Bureau of the Census Supplementary Report PC (S1)-47, July 28, 1965; John Radzilowski, "A Survey of Polish Americans: The 1980 Census," unpublished report, June 1987, in author's possession; Radzilowski, "Location of the Polish American Population, 1980–1990," 2–3; U.S. Census published statistics, 1860–2000; Minnesota State Census, 1905; F. Niklewicz, *Polacy w Stanach Zjednoczonych;* 2000 Census numbers given are upper-boundary estimates.

Nordeast, p. 18: Joseph Hart, "Notes of a Native Son," *City Pages,* Aug. 13, 1997, 12–18; Northeast Neighborhood House Records, Box 4, Head Worker's Reports, Sept. 1917; Frank Rog, *Let Me Be Frank* (Minneapolis, 2003), 25, 9; Zak Kieley, *Heart and Hard Work,* 128.

Symphonies of Stone and Stained Glass, p. 28: Thaddeus Radzilowski, "The View from a Polish Ghetto: Some Observations on the First One Hundred Years in Detroit," *Ethnicity* 1 (July 1974): 125–50 (quote); Richard Wolniewicz, "Comparative Ethnic Church Architecture," *Polish American Studies* 54 (Spring 1997): 53–73; Dennis Kolinski, "Shrines and Crosses in Rural Central Wisconsin," *Polish American Studies* 51 (Autumn 1994): 33; Geoffrey M. Gyrisco, "Victor Kordela and the Architecture of Polish and East-Slavic Identity in America," *Polish American Studies* 54 (Spring 1997): 33–52; *Church of the Holy Cross, 1886–1986;* John Radziłowski, "Polish American Architecture in

Comparative Perspective" (introduction to special issue), *Polish American Studies* 54 (Spring 1997): 5–8. Kordela was probably also partly responsible for the decoration (and perhaps the design as well) of St. John Cantius in Wilno.

The Polish American Press in Minnesota, p. 48: Kruszka, *History of Poles in America to 1908,* 1:275-76. *Wiarus* is variously translated as "the old guard," "the old campaigner," or "the old veteran," but the author has chose "the faithful one," which is more in keeping with the sense of the word's root in (Polish "wiara" or faith) and with the mission and general editorial line of the newspaper. Its general pro-Catholic stance was also reflected in its brief name change to *Katolik* (The Catholic) and its masthead symbol that combined both religious and national imagery.

Stan Wasie: Pioneer of Overnight Shipping, p. 59: Wasie Foundation files, including newspaper clippings, copies of public documents, and a few short biographical articles, especially ones put together for Wasie's posthumous induction into the Minnesota Business Hall of Fame. *Minneapolis Tribune,* Mar. 9, 1967; *Minneapolis Star,* May 11, 1956; *Shakopee Valley News,* Sept. 26, 1957, p. 9, 12; *Star Tribune,* Oct. 17, 1992, p.1B.

At the Table with Poles in Minnesota,

p. 68: Thaddeus C. Radzilowski, "Immigrant Women and Their Daughters," 22; Ken Parejko, *Remember Me Dancing* (Oregon, Wis., 1996), 21–27 (hog butchering); Radziłowski, "Hidden Cosmos," 147–49, 182–83 (making whiskey).

Something of Their Very Own to Say, p. 74: Thomas Gladsky, "Monika Krawczyk, Victoria Janda, and the Polanie Club," and Bernard Koloski, "Children's Books: Lois Lenski, Maia Wojciechowska, Anne Pellowski," in *Something of My Very Own to Say,* 100–127 (quote), 144–69. See also *Our Minnesota* 1, no. 8 (June 1941): 40; *Minneapolis Star,* May 17, 1951, p. 40, Nov. 1, 1954, p.18; *Minneapolis Tribune,* April 2, 1961, p.13B, Nov. 2, 1954, p.17. Victor Contoski, ed., *Blood of their Blood: An Anthology of Polish-American Poetry* (St. Paul, 1980); John Minczeski, ed., *Concert at Chopin's House: A Collection of Polish-American Writing* (St. Paul, 1987). Contoski is the son of Josepha Contoski, a founding member of Polanie Club. Janda's three collections are *Star Hunger* (1942), *Walls of Space* (1945), and *Singing Furrows* (1952). Minczeski's works include *Spiders* (1979), *Reconstruction of Light* (1981), *Gravity* (1991), and *Circle Routes* (2001). Nowak's works include *Revenants* (2000). Rezmerski's works include *What Do I Know?* (2000) and *Held for Questioning* (1969).

Index

Page numbers in italic refer to pictures and captions.

Picture Credits

Names of the photographers, when known, are in parentheses.

Page 41, 7 (both), 49—Polish Museum of Winona, Winona, Minn.

Page x, 11, 13, 23, 24, 26, 30, 33, 34, 42, 46, 47, 51, 52, 60 (Chet Janas Studio), 62 (Schomadter), 69, 70, 80—Polish American Collection, Immigration History Research Cen-ter, University of Minnesota

Page 9, 28, 29, 31, 36 (Steven C. Trimble), 37, 55 (Kregel Photo Parlors), 56 (Franklin F. Holbrook), 61, 67 (Paul Iida), 71 (*St. Paul Dispatch and Pioneer Press*)—

Minnesota Historical Society

Page 20, 21—Gregory F. Kishel

Page 45, 75 (Wieslaw Suszynski), 77—John Radzilowski

Page 59—The Wasie Foundation

Page 72—courtesy of Emeline Dziabas Cook

Acknowledgments

This book could not have been written without the support and encouragement of many people. My father, Prof. Thaddeus C. Radzilowski, and my friend and mentor, Prof. Joseph Amato, inspired me to look at places and people around me with a historian's eye. Prof. Brian Gratton, Arizona State University, critiqued and improved early versions of the research. Members of the Polish Genealogical Society of Minnesota were a constant source of facts and ideas. Particular thanks goes to the tireless work of Paul Kulas and Greg Kishel. My editor at Minnesota Historical Society Press, Sally Rubinstein, was a model of calm and dedication who gently squeezed a longer book into the more compact and readable result you hold in your hand. Many individuals in Minnesota and Poland provided photos, documents, and other necessary materials, including Danuta Pytlak (University of Warsaw), Wieslaw and Elzbieta Suszynski (Adam Mickiewicz Polish Saturday School), Czesław Róg (Pol-Am Newsletter), Fr. Paul Breza (Polish Museum of Winona), Megan McCluskey of Vision Design Group in Winona, the staff of the Immigration History Research Center at the University of Minnesota, and Jan Louwagie of the Southwest Minnesota Regional Research Center. I will be forever grateful to the many Polish Americans across Minnesota who provided me with their memories, allowed me to rummage through their church basements and wander through their cemeteries, and told me stories of past and present. Special thanks goes to Rose Parulski of Ivanhoe and the late Paul Libera of Winona who collected and preserved local history long before it was popular. Finally, I thank Katarzyna Polanska who was with me as I wrote each page and to whom this book is dedicated with love and gratitude.

Minnesotans can trace their families and their state's heritage to a multitude of ethnic groups. *The People of Minnesota* series tells each group's story in a compact, handsomely illustrated, and accessible paperback. Readers will learn about the group's accomplishments, ethnic organizations, settlement patterns, and occupations. Each book includes a personal story of one person or family, told through a diary, a letter, or an oral history.

In his introduction to the series, Bill Holm reminds us why these stories are as important as ever: "To be ethnic, somehow, is to be human. Neither can we escape it, nor should we want to. You cannot interest yourself in the lives of your neighbors if you don't take sufficient interest in your own."

This series is based on the critically acclaimed book *They Chose Minnesota: A Survey of the State's Ethnic Groups* (Minnesota Historical Society Press). The volumes in *The People of Minnesota* bring each group's story up to date and add dozens of photographs to inform and enhance the telling.

Books in the series include *Irish in Minnesota*, *Jews in Minnesota*, *Norwegians in Minnesota*, *African Americans in Minnesota*, *Germans in Minnesota*, *Chinese in Minnesota*, and *Swedes in Minnesota*.

Bill Holm is the grandson of four Icelandic immigrants to Minneota, Minnesota, where he still lives. He is the author of eight books including *Eccentric Island: Travels Real and Imaginary* and *Coming Home Crazy*. When he is not practicing the piano or on the road circuit-riding for literature, he teaches at Southwest State University in Marshall, Minnesota.

About the Author

John Radzilowski is a senior fellow at Piast Institute: A National Center for Polish and Polish American Affairs, Detroit, Mich.; president of the Polish American Cultural Institute of Minnesota; and the author of books and articles on Polish Americans.